ABCs of Costume Jewelry

Advice for Buying and Collecting

Dave & Lee Salsbery

Schiffer Publishing Ltd®

4880 Lower Valley Road, Atglen, PA 19310 USA

Dedication

We dedicate this book to our dear friend
and mentor, Henri Dill

Designed by Mark David Bowyer
Type set in Benguiat BT bolded/Aldine 721 BT

ISBN: 0-7643-1913-2
Printed in China
1 2 3 4

Published by Schiffer Publishing Ltd.
4880 Lower Valley Road
Atglen, PA 19310
Phone: (610) 593-1777; Fax: (610) 593-2002
E-mail: Schifferbk@aol.com
Please visit our web site catalog at **www.schifferbooks.com**
We are always looking for people to write books on new and related subjects. If you have an idea for a book, please contact us at the above address.

This book may be purchased from the publisher.
Include $3.95 for shipping. Please try your bookstore first.
You may write for a free catalog.

In Europe, Schiffer books are distributed by
Bushwood Books
6 Marksbury Ave. Kew Gardens
Surrey TW9 4JF England
Phone: 44 (0)20 8392-8585; Fax: 44 (0)20 8392-9876
E-mail: Bushwd@aol.com
Free postage in the UK. Europe: air mail at cost.
Please try your bookstore first.

Contents

Advice 5

Buying: Basics To Know 6
Signed Costume Jewelry 23
How Much Is It Worth? 40
The Rhinestones 41
Metals and Finishes 44
Things to Consider 48
Where To Get The Best Buys? 52

Collecting: What to Choose? 64
What the Professionals Kept: 71
    Figural Jewelry 71
    Signed Jewelry 73
    Unsigned Jewelry 79
An Avid Collector's Inspiring Choices: 84
    Compacts 84
    Crowns 85
    Christmas Jewelry 90
    Patriotic Jewelry 91
    Butterflies 92
    Signed Jewelry 94
    Unsigned Jewelry 121
A Passionate Collector's Broad Interests: ... 127
    Marcel Boucher Jewelry 127
    Figural Jewelry 135
    Signed Jewelry 143
    Unsigned Jewelry 159

Clean, Display, and Protect 172
Recommended Reading 175
Index of Designers 176

Acknowledgments

We thank hundreds of customers who purchased items of jewelry from us over the years. You gave us the experiences we would draw from to write this book. Most of you became our friends, and now that we have retired, we miss the time we spent with you.

Our thanks also go to Chris Palmer, Don Wirfs, and the staff of Palmer/Wirfs for providing us the opportunity to participate in the antique shows they promote on the West Coast.

Special thanks go to Dean Mathews, Barbara Satalino, and Henri Dill, who made their jewelry collections available for photography and gave of their time while we wrote descriptions of each item. Henri was there, with support and encouragement every step of the way, when we started our costume jewelry business. Her positive attitude and sunny disposition never wavers. She and her husband, Ernie, own Engleberg Antiks in Salem, Oregon. Thanks also to Anne Kaufman who let us photograph her wonderful matching set by David Andersen.

Values

The values in this book may vary by the collection. The values, circa dates, and descriptions are based on information provided by each collector. They are provided for general information purposes only.

The authors, publisher, or collectors assume no responsibility for any losses that might be incurred as a result of consulting this guide.

Advice

To make this a personal message to our readers, we refer to ourselves as Dave and Lee. Several years prior to retiring from the business world, we discussed our future and decided we wanted something to do together. Dave was a Certified Public Accountant and Lee was a Registered Nurse. Neither of us wanted to do anything related to our prior work. Because we had friends in the antique business, we began to look at that as a possibility.

Neither of us had any knowledge of antiques, so Lee began visiting local antique malls to get an idea of what they were selling. With that limited knowledge, she began buying small items here and there at garage and antique sales. The first items were inexpensive but covered a wide range of categories, including a small amount of costume jewelry.

When we had enough merchandise, Lee rented space in a local antique mall. It was discouraging at first, because sales were low and often not enough to pay the rent. The owner of the mall suggested we consider selling our goods at antique shows.

We must have been crazy. Our first show was a large one in San Francisco, California, at the Cow Palace. We paid over $200 for a small space, traveled more than 1,000 miles, rented a motel for five nights, and paid to eat in restaurants the entire time. Our sales totaled $700. Do we need to tell you whether we made a profit?

But we learned from this experience. We loved the travel, eating out in new restaurants, and visiting new places in the bay area. Lee especially enjoyed meeting new people and was an instant hit with the customers. It was evident, after the first show, who would be the public relations and sales person. Dave loved to search for bargains, so he became the primary buyer.

After that first show, we made some decisions. Although we lost money, most of the dealers we talked to had made money and we felt we could, too. We did not like taking large items to shows, as it was inconvenient and they took up so much space. That is when we decided to specialize in costume jewelry and related items. Soon, without knowing it, we also became costume jewelry collectors.

Lee bought every jewelry book she could find on the subject and studied them to learn more. We visited many antique stores and went to antique shows to increase our knowledge. We probably asked too many dumb questions but we continued buying and started our new career.

After buying, repairing, and selling thousands of pieces, over the next few years, we learned from our mistakes so that eventually our sales for a three-day show became over $20,000.

We share this story to give you the basis for our thinking. We may have learned something that we can share with you. For fifteen years, we specialized in costume jewelry and became very successful. We took time to listen to, and answer, the questions of our customers. From this, we learned what information could be helpful to others. During the time, we were buying jewelry for resale and adding to our personal collections, our purchases numbered in the thousands. While Dave was buying, Lee was cleaning and repairing.

In this book, we hope to provide information that will help you avoid many of the mistakes we made and improve your purchasing skills. Since this is only a beginning, we have also provided a list of reference books you may use to increase your knowledge.

Buying:
Basics To Know

When you start any new endeavor, you need some basic knowledge to feel comfortable discussing it, asking questions, and reading about it. Please excuse us if this section seems basic; we will use these terms throughout the book and want everyone to be familiar with them. We will give you a very basic overview of costume jewelry and hope you will become familiar with the terms.

In this section, we take you on an imaginary visit to a large antiques show and guide you through a visit to a jewelry booth. Increased knowledge will greatly improve your ability to ask informed questions.

During our shows, we were asked unbelievable questions. As one lady looked at our display of several hundred pieces, she said, "Did you make all of this jewelry?" Another lady looked at our large rhinestone collection and asked, "Are those all diamonds?" Another just asked if they were all "real." Reading this section would not have made them experts, but it would have certainly improved the quality of their questions.

When you visit a jewelry booth at an antique show and look at their prices, remember that the dealer paid hundreds of dollars for show space, traveled to the show, rented motels for several nights, and paid to eat out in order to bring you the jewelry you see. All of this cost must be covered, in part, by the price of the jewelry.

As you approach the booth and look into the cases, you will notice a large variety of jewelry. If the dealer has "**real**" (diamonds, gold, etc.) jewelry, it will usually be separated from the "**costume**" (imitation) jewelry and will be in locked cases. The first thing you may notice are small signs with names on them. These are the names of the designers or companies that created the costume jewelry. If you examine the pieces near these signs, you should find the names of the designers or makers imprinted ("**signed**") in the metal on the back of the jewelry.

Dealers showcase with signs identifying the various designers who created the jewelry.

The Stones

As you look at the jewelry, you will see that a large number of pieces have clear and/or colored stones. You can be sure that these are not real gemstones because of their size, if nothing else. For the most part, these are crystal, or in other words glass, many of which probably originated in Austria. These are commonly called "**rhinestones**". The name most commonly recognized in the manufacture of these stones today is Swarovski.

The Settings

As you look closely at the pieces, you will note that the stones are "set" (held in place) in one of two different ways. The larger stones are almost always held in place by four or more small metal prongs that are bent up around the stone, somewhat like you find in gemstone jewelry. This method is called "**prong set**." Smaller stones are usually sunk into the metal, have no prongs to hold them, and are glued in. This method is called "**pave' set**."

Example of prong set, open back settings. This sterling brooch is an Eisenberg Original. Clear pavé set rhinestones covering the leaf design metal with a light gold wash. Perfect nearly 2" open back, prong set lavender stone. Piece is near perfect but appears it may have had a professional conversion from a fur clip. c. 1930s. Authors' Collection. $250-350

Example of pavé set rhinestones on this lovely signed Jomaz brooch. Shown with signed earrings but notice they are not a set. Courtesy of Engleberg Antiks. c.1960s. Pin $55-65. Earrings $25-30

Example of large blue and clear closed-back rhinestones in a signed Yves St. Laurent necklace. c.1960s. Authors' Collection. $225-275

Back of necklace shows the silver metal completely covers the stones.

Large 4" unsigned Trifari brooch of a water bird completely covered with clear pavé set rhinestones and one large green open back center stone. Three dimension effect with head and neck of bird raised and curved. c.1960s Authors' Collection. $175-225

The Backs

If you pick up one of the jewelry pieces and turn it over, you will notice that some of the stones are uncovered in the back. On others, the metal is smooth and covers the back of the stone so the back cannot be seen. The first are referred to as "**open back**" stones and the latter, "**closed back**." Stones were frequently covered on the back side with a very thin, foil-like coating to make them more reflective. Pave-set stones almost always have **foil backs**. Open back stones may or may not have foil backs. If they do, you will be able to see the foil on the back of the stone.

Back of water bird brooch shows good example of open foil back stone.

Iridescent Stones

Aside from the color of the stones, you may notice that some have a slight iridescent glaze on the surface. These stones are referred to as having an **"aurora borealis"** finish, or **"a. b."** for short.

Aurora Borealis stones are illustrated in this almost 3" long signed Weiss Butterfly pin with 1.5" long matching earrings. Pin has mix of blue and green prong-set rhinestones (some aurora borealis) in japanned (blackened) metal. Authors' Collection. c.1950s. $95-125

The Shapes of Stones

We don't want to be technical when discussing the various attributes of stones, so we will be very brief. The surface of most rhinestones is cut similar to gemstones leaving small flat reflective surfaces or "**facets**." The cut stones actually have a small flat surface (**table**) on top and are pointed on the bottom. Looking down from the top you will notice the various shapes of the stones. Most of the rhinestones in costume jewelry are probably "**round cut**." If these have many reflective surfaces or facets they are called "**diamond cut**." The next most popular shape is probably the "**marquise cut**" (also called "**navette**") that is generally rounded but comes to a point on both ends. The narrow rect-angular shaped stones are "**baguettes**." The square stones with the corners removed are "**emerald cut**." You also will find "**pear** or **tear drop**" rhinestones and many other shaped stones not mentioned here. Round or oval shaped stones that are rounded on the top and have *no facets* are "**cabochons**." Most rhinestones are faceted on the backs. Others are flat and are referred to as "**flat backs**." Flat back stones are seldom found in better costume jewelry, except when large open back stones were used. A few jewelry designers, Schreiner for example, would sometimes mount the rhinestones in reverse with the pointed backside in front for dramatic effect.

Example of prong-set, round-cut rhinestones used to complete this unsigned, 7" long, link bracelet. Courtesy of Engleberg Antiks. c.1950-'60s. $45-65

Marquise shaped, clear, prong-set rhinestones in a single row are used exclusively in this unsigned bracelet, complete with safety chain. Courtesy of Engleberg Antiks. c.1950s-'60s. $55-65

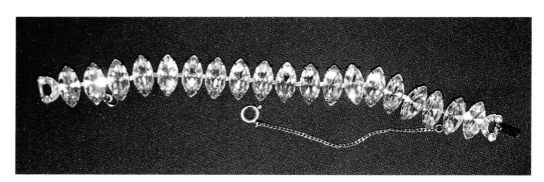

Dozens of baguette and round, clear, prong-set rhinestones are used in the construction of this wonderful, double-hinged, cuff bracelet. The combination of layered rhinestones in a rhodium finish makes this an elegant, unsigned bracelet. Authors' Collection. c.1940s. $175-225

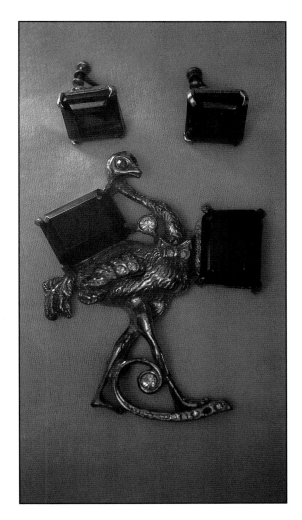

Large, square-cut, emerald green rhinestones are set in heavy gold finished metal in this 3.5" long, unsigned, ostrich brooch with matching earrings. Courtesy of Engleberg Antiks. c.1930s. $65-75

The Fasteners

Pieces of jewelry with pin backs are referred to as "**pins**" or "**brooches**." We normally use brooch to refer to the larger and better pieces. When you pick up a brooch and turn it over you may not find a pin as expected. If instead, it has two long hinged prongs, it is not a brooch but is a "**fur clip**." These were originally made to wear on furs but may be worn on most heavy fabrics. They are not good to wear on silk or light materials: first, because they poke holes in the cloth and second, because they are usually too heavy. If the piece has a hinged flat metal piece on the back, instead of a pin, it is a "**dress clip**." These were made to wear on a dress but must be clipped over the top of the neckline or a pocket. Most of the fur clips and dress clips were made before 1940. Sometimes you will find a brooch complete with a pin but on a framework that holds two identical fur or dress clips together. They can be worn as one piece or, when the framework is removed, worn separately. This type of jewelry is usually associated with and may have been made by the Coro Company. It is commonly called a "**duette**" regardless of who made it.

A single, large, green cabochon is used in this gold finished, cross pin/pendant signed Hobé. Courtesy Engleberg Antiks. c.1970s. $55-65

A newer, 2" long, gold finished elephant pin is shown with an older, c.1930s, pair of silver, 2.5" long, dress clips. Both are signed "Joseff." Courtesy of Engleberg Antiks. Elephant $100-125. Pair dress clips $75-100

Reverse side of the Joseff dress clips. The large flat clip must be clipped over a pocket or neckline to fasten it to the garment.

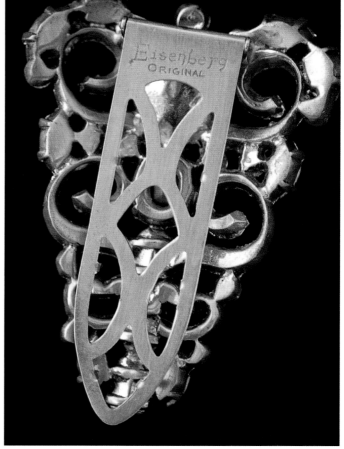

This is a signed, Eisenberg Original, dress clip with large, clear rhinestones and a silver finish. It is in great condition for its age. c.1930s. Authors' Collection. $350-450

Reverse of the Eisenberg Original dress clip.

This wonderful, over 3" long fur clip is signed
Eisenberg Original. It has large, clear rhine-
stones and a nice, silver finish. c.1930s.
Authors' Collection. $450-550

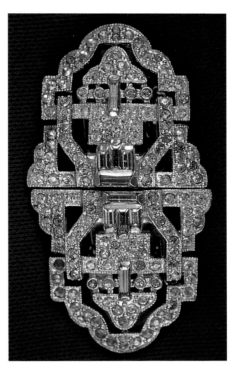

This piece, which appears to be a brooch,
is a duette from the 1930s. Authors
Collection. $65-85

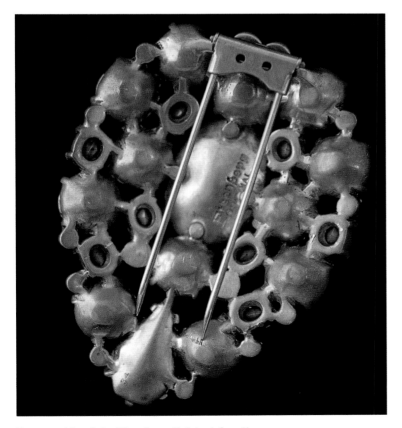

Reverse side of the Eisenberg Original fur clip.
Note the double prongs that must be inserted into
the fabric of the garment to fasten it. Made to wear
on fur, but can be worn on any heavy material.

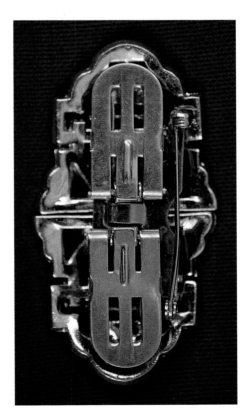

This is the reverse of the duette,
showing the pin when it is worn as
one piece.

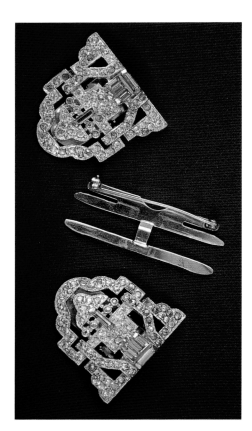

This is the front of the duette when it is separated from the frame and is now two dress clips.

Other Types of Silver Jewelry

Silver jewelry includes other fairly large groups. Many of the pieces you will see may have been made in **Mexico** or be of **Native American** origin. The Native American silver is usually easily identifiable by its distinctive design. The Mexican jewelry is usually marked "Mexico," "**Taxco**," or other place of origin and is stamped "925." Certain of these pieces can be very valuable when stamped with the right designer's name. If you are interested in collecting silver jewelry, there are several books on that subject.

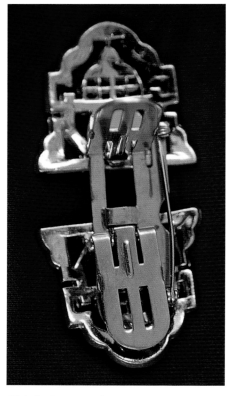

This is the back of the duette showing how the two dress clips slide into the frame to put it back together as one piece.

The Metals

Rhinestone jewelry has been made from any number of less expensive metals and is usually finished with a light gold or silver coating. However applied, the finishes are usually made to last and with proper care will outlive the owner. Some jewelry was made from sterling silver, but in many cases with a gold coating or wash applied so the jewelry does not look like sterling. These pieces are normally stamped "**sterling**." Sterling is a mixture of 925 parts refined silver and 75 parts copper. Jewelry that is marked "**925**" is "**sterling silver**."

If you look at some of the better pieces of costume jewelry, you will find they are just as nice on the back as they are on the front. Many of these have a rhodium finish, which has a silver appearance and is probably one of the nicest finishes found on costume jewelry, because it will not tarnish. A few of the older pieces that are beautiful on the front were made out of a cheap metal referred to as "**pot metal**." These pieces usually have dull backs that look like they never had a finish coating. Regardless of the metal used in the construction they may still be very collectible, if in good condition.

This is an unusual alpaca design on a sterling bracelet signed "Velstria Perlana 925" with the initials "SF." Authors' Collection. $135-150

An example of the many sterling pins signed Hobé. This small 2" pin, smaller than most, is a bow with leaf and seed pod design. Larger signed Hobé sterling pins of this type design are worth much more. Courtesy of Engleberg Antiks. c.1930s. $45-65

An newer, unsigned, 2" long, mechanical bicycle pendant with box chain. The sterling pendant is fascinating because the wheels turn and the front wheel can be steered by moving the handlebars. Authors' Collection. c.1970s. $75-100

Good workmanship in this 2" wide, sterling, cuff bracelet with turquoise stones. Signed "Mexico" and designer's initials. Nice sample of current Mexican jewelry. Authors' Collection. c.1990s. $60-80

Large black onyx stones stand out in the sterling silver metal with a background of tiny, pavé-set marcasite stones. It is unsigned, but still a beautiful older necklace. c.1930s-1940s. Authors' Collection. $150-175

Other sterling pieces marked "**Siam**" were brought back to the U.S. by soldiers returning from the Asian theater in the Second World War. These are usually narrow bracelets or smaller pins that have black and white enamel with designs of dancers. Siam silver is usually inexpensive, except for larger bracelets and necklaces or items finished in other colors.

Sterling pieces from Norway, Denmark, and a few other countries also appear on the market. These are usually made with fine silver, are frequently signed by the maker, and may be more valuable than some other silver pieces. An example is the fine matching set by David Andersen.

The original case this set came in is stamped "David Andersen Juveleer." Each piece is signed "David Andersen, Christiania, Norway." Christiania became Oslo in 1924. This wonderful set was designed to be worn in Norwegian ceremonies. Dated 1881. Courtesy of Anne Kaufman. $900-1200

Close-up photos show the fine detail and workmanship. The metal appears to be a higher percent of silver than found in sterling (925/100).

Close-up of the brooch.

Close-up of the bracelet

Copper Jewelry

You will easily recognize copper jewelry by its rich brown color. Many of the better copper pieces have an area of enameled finish on the front. The most plentiful of these are signed "**Matisse**", "**Renoir**", or both. By far the most valuable copper jewelry is marked "**Rebajes**." The condition of the enameled finish and rarity of the piece greatly affect its value.

A wide copper bracelet with large matching pin signed "Copper Bell." Although they have nice construction and attention to detail, their value is not high because they lack an enameled finish. Courtesy of Engleberg Antiks. c.1950s. Each $20-25

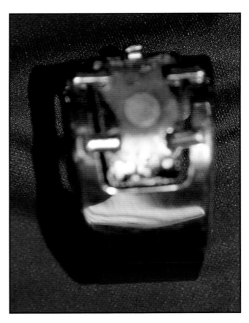

This signed Matisse cuff bracelet in copper has some very interesting enameled highlights. Courtesy of Engleberg Antiks. c.1950s. $65-75

This copper painter's pallet pin, with matching earrings, is one of the well known and recognizable sets signed "Renoir." The enameled finish is still perfect, which enhances the value. Courtesy of Engleberg Antiks. $85-95

The enamel on this copper piece, by Renoir, is in excellent condition. Even with the good enameled finish and signature, it has limited popularity today because of the white color. Courtesy of Engleberg Antiks. c.1950s. $35-45

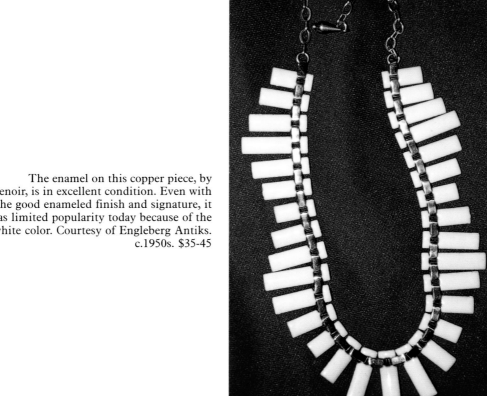

Plastic Jewelry

Many dealers will have some plastic jewelry in their cases. There are many avid collectors of plastic jewelry, especially that originated by the Bakelite Company. **Bakelite** is readily identifiable by the chemical smell omitted when it is heated. The easiest and most accurate way to test it is to run hot water over the piece and smell it while it is hot. If you are going to collect plastic jewelry, we suggest you read a book specializing on that subject.

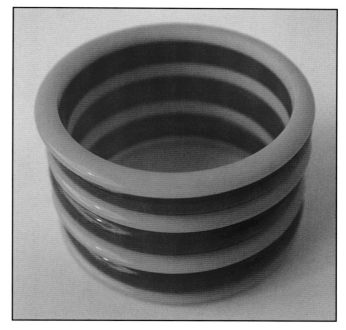

A stack of four yellow and three red Bakelite bangle bracelets. Bakelite is usually worn in "nests," as shown. These were all found in a plastic bag at a garage sale. c.1930s. $175-220

Three carved bangle bracelets made of plastics. Two are Bakelite. Cannot tell which one is not? You must learn how to recognize and test these. Courtesy Engleberg Antiks. c.1930s. Plastic $10-15. Bakelite each $95-100

Black and white Bakelite necklace with matching earrings with a dainty carved rose design. Set is signed "Germany." Courtesy of Engleberg Antiks. c.1930s. $125-150

Light pink, green, red, and blue leaves and fruit combined in a 15" long strand of pink beads form an attractive necklace with a spring look. Pierced 2.5" long earrings match it perfectly. Necklace is a little short, but this is a nice plastic set and is collectible because of its "Carmen Miranda" look, even though it is not Bakelite. Authors' Collection. c.1980s. $75-95

Faux Pearls

Among this jewelry, you will find pi!eces that have "faux" or man-made pearls in their construction. They have a thin, shiny coating that gives them the "real pearl" look. Faux pearls are used individually and strung in single and multiple strands. Jewelry with pearls often have ornate decorations made with a combination of pearls, rhinestones, and metal leaves or other decorations held together by fine strands of wire. Ornate and expensive pieces with pearls may be signed by Miriam Haskell, DeMario, Robert, Eugene, and Hagler. You will also see pearl strands and bracelets that are much older, having been given as engagement gifts, prior to 1940, and came in gift boxes. Strands of faux pearls may have very nice sterling clasps. We had little market for older strands of pearls, but often sold the more ornate presentation boxes for $100 to $700.

The single strand of faux pearls is unusual in that it is signed "Hobé." It is a very nice, 20" long strand with perfect faux pearls separated by tiny metal beads. Courtesy of Engleberg Antiks. c.1950s. $95-105

The single-strand choker of faux pearls is of little value. Although nice and very wearable, note the almost transparent pearls with no beads or knots between them. The three-strand, faux pearl bracelet is also in good condition but, like the choker, is not knotted or separated by beads. It does, however, have a nice clasp with rhinestones. Courtesy of Engleberg Antiks. c.1950s. Each $45-55

Nice single strand of 20" Haskell pearls signed on the clasp as well as the small metal hang tag. Note the small metal findings between the pearls always found on Haskell pearls. Courtesy of Engleberg Antiks. c.1950s. $95-135

Faux pearl set signed by Stanley Hagler. It is finished with dozens of tiny faux pearls, in an intricate design, with nice, gold-colored, metal and large pearl-like drops that dangle. A nice set in perfect condition. Authors' Collection. $550-650

This is a lovely, three-strand, faux pearl choker. It is finely designed, with small clear rhinestones in the clasp and centerpiece. It is highlighted by a large, faux emerald center stone. Probably came in a presentation case as an engagement gift in the 1920s or 1930s. Authors' Collection. $75-125

Beads

A dealer may have strands of beads in their display. These will vary somewhat in price, depending on the cut of the beads, what they are made of, and how well they are strung. Beads may be metal, bone, ivory, amber, shell or other materials, including plastics or glass. Glass beads, as well as rhinestones, may have the aurora borealis (a. b.) finish. Plastic beads, other than those made of Bakelite, or those in Carmen Miranda (colorful fruit and flower shapes) style, are usually low in value.

Clasp of necklace

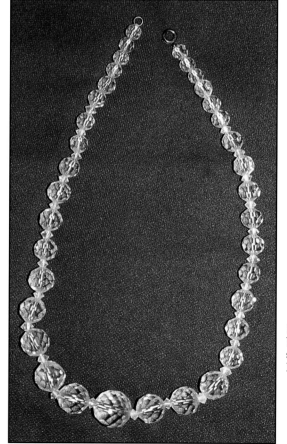

Large clear glass beads separated by tiny black beads are striking. A quality set of beads with a very nice clasp with clear rhinestones. Probably a newer necklace. Courtesy of Engleberg Antiks. $45-55

Short choker length strand of clear graduated size glass beads with a sterling clasp. This strands light weight and smooth facets make it comfortable to wear. Courtesy of Engleberg Antiks. $55-65

Signed Costume Jewelry

Costume jewelry is referred to as "signed" when it has an individual designer's name, company name, or logo imprinted in some way on the piece. Some people would also include, in that definition, pieces marked with the place of origin or marks such as Sterling or 925 identifying the metal.

The signature, whatever type it may be, is usually marked in the metal on the back of a brooch, for example, in an open flat area. It may, however, be imprinted on the staff of the fastening pin. On a necklace or bracelet, it is usually on the back of the clasp, but may be on a link, or sometimes on every link, of the piece. Sometimes a metal tag is attached near the clasp that may include the only signature on the piece. In the case of jewelry made by Miriam Haskell, the tag and the clasp are usually stamped with her signature. If you check one piece of a set for the designer's name and do not find it, check the other pieces, too. Sometimes only one piece of a set is signed. If all of the pieces in a set do not contain the signature, examine the design of the pieces carefully, as they may not belong together.

Since the signatures are on the backs of the jewelry, they may have become worn over time and be difficult to read. Also, the signature is often too small to read. For that reason, and others that will become obvious later, we suggest that you invest in a jewelry "**loupe**," or other type of magnifying device, you can easily carry with you. These may be obtained in various magnifications and are relatively inexpensive. Maybe our eyes are wearing out, but we prefer a 16-power loupe; you may be satisfied with one that is 8- or 10-power. You can purchase these at stationary stores, jewelry supply stores, or jewelry supply booths at an antiques show.

When you are looking at a piece of jewelry, you should turn it over and look for a signature. Look also at the design and if it has a signature relate the design to the signature. In time, you will become able to look at a piece and know what the signature should be before you pick it up. We used to make a game of this. When we saw a piece, we would both guess the name of the designer and then turn it over to see who was correct. To find the signature, hold the piece so the light shines across the metal so you can detect indentations or rough-looking areas.

Two inch wide signed Laguna clip earrings with a 14" three strand clear crystal necklace. Nice findings and workmanship. Beads, like these, are not very popular as they are heavy and the facets on the beads make them slightly abrasive to the skin. Courtesy of Engleberg Antiks. $65-75

Shown are 16 power loupe and smaller 10 power loupe. These fold and fit easily in the pocket or purse and are essential if you are buying costume jewelry.

Sometimes the name will be obvious; if not, examine it further with your loupe. Once you become familiar with a specific designer's signature, you will know where to find it on their pieces, as most designers were consistent in where they applied it. Now that you have found the signature and determined who it is, you may wonder what value that information is to you.

First, the signature tells you the designer or manufacturer.

Now, this is easy if ,for instance, it says Eisenberg, Weiss, or Hollycraft. But, what if it is a script E or maybe just a small design that was the logo of a company? It takes a little research to learn what some of these things mean. We suggest that you write down the signatures or logos that are new to you, and look them up when you get home.

We have included photos of several pieces of signed jewelry. Each is by a different designer and is a piece fairly representative of their jewelry.

This brooch is signed "Joseff Hollywood". It has a heavy gold finish over a dainty metal leaf pattern with heavily cut graduated size clear rhinestones around a large deep blue center stone. c.1950s. Authors' Collection. $375-475

Large clear emerald cut rhinestones form this wide signed Weiss necklace with matching clip earrings. This is a very nice set. Authors' Collection. $300-450

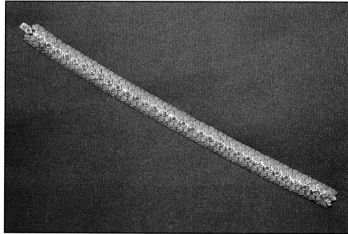

Very fine flexible 7" bracelet by Ciner. Tiny red and blue stones are set in a gold finish metal. Ciner bracelets have very tiny links and are the most flexible of any we've found. Authors' Collection. c.1960s. $250-350

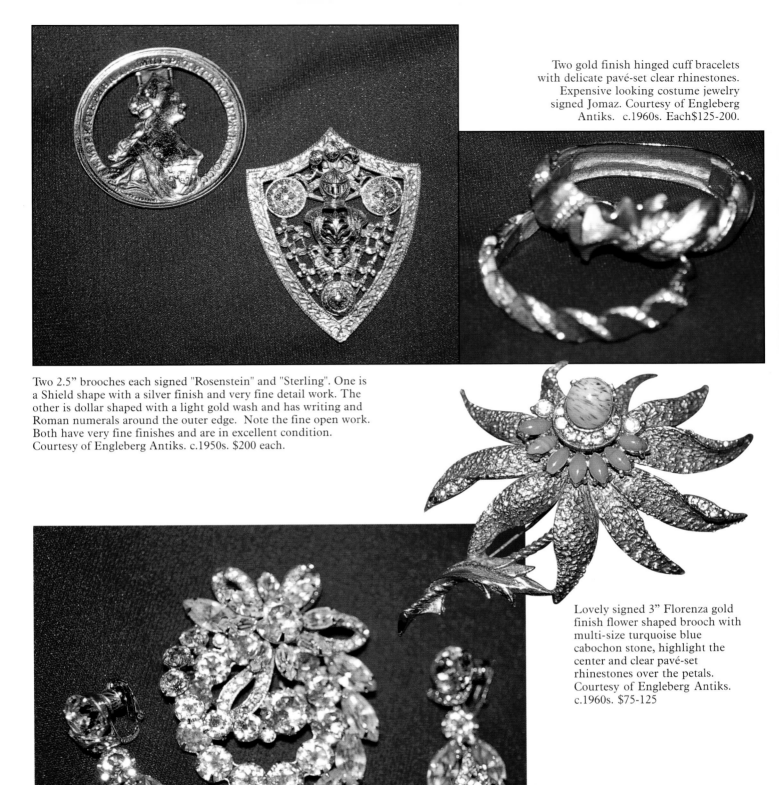

Two gold finish hinged cuff bracelets with delicate pavé-set clear rhinestones. Expensive looking costume jewelry signed Jomaz. Courtesy of Engleberg Antiks. c.1960s. Each $125-200.

Two 2.5" brooches each signed "Rosenstein" and "Sterling". One is a Shield shape with a silver finish and very fine detail work. The other is dollar shaped with a light gold wash and has writing and Roman numerals around the outer edge. Note the fine open work. Both have very fine finishes and are in excellent condition. Courtesy of Engleberg Antiks. c.1950s. $200 each.

Lovely signed 3" Florenza gold finish flower shaped brooch with multi-size turquoise blue cabochon stone, highlight the center and clear pavé-set rhinestones over the petals. Courtesy of Engleberg Antiks. c.1960s. $75-125

Signed Eisenberg brooch with matching clip earrings. Multi-layer construction, with many different size prong and pavé-set clear rhinestones, form this elegant design. Excellent condition. Courtesy of Engleberg Antiks. c.1940s-50s. $150-175

Second, you will be able to determine its approximate age.

As you become more familiar with the signatures, and look them up, you will not only know who made the piece, but will have some idea of when the piece was made. Hollycraft Corporation was one of the few companies that, not only put their name on most of their jewelry, but the date as well. Others seldom included the date but you can learn the approximate age by knowing when the company was in business or when they used a certain signature. For instance, the Eisenberg Company used several different signatures over the years. The script E and Eisenberg Original were their earlier pre 1940s marks. In the 1940s they started using Eisenberg in block letters and then Eisenberg Ice. When you cannot tell the age of a piece by the signature, you may be able to tell it by the design or the materials it is made of.

Third, the signature will make it easier to approximate the value.

A signed piece can be compared to other similar pieces by the same designer. Remember, however, the condition of the pieces you compare must be similar.

Fourth, knowing signatures will make you more confident.

A knowledge of "signatures" will add to your enjoyment of collecting and will put you in the "know", as you might say, with other collectors and dealers. You will be able to ask more intelligent questions and discuss the pieces with them. After a short time, you begin to picture the jewelry in your mind, when you hear the designer's name.

For just a minute, let us consider how having a signature on a piece of costume jewelry affects its value. If you have all of the pieces from any one designer laid out on a table what will you find? No matter who the designer is, you will find some high-end pieces. You will always find some of lower quality. It might be fair to say that signatures alone do not make a piece valuable. A signed piece must be in good condition and be of quality design and construction to be of relatively high value.

Look at the following pieces of Eisenberg jewelry that illustrate the variety in both style and quality that is sold by a company over a period of time.

Small 1.25 inch fur clip signed "Eisenberg Original". It is in very good condition with a variety of shapes of clear rhinestones. Value on this piece is low due to its size. Courtesy of Engleberg Antiks. c.1930s-40s. $125-175

This is a large signed sterling Eisenberg brooch. It has a combination of clear pavé and prong set rhinestones. It has a large clear prong set center stone in a design which appears to be a combination bow and flower. c.1930s-40s. Authors' Collection. $350-450

Long signed Eisenberg brooch with large matching clip earrings. This brooch is representative of the multi-layer construction found in finer Eisenberg pieces. Clear and pavé-set rhinestones. Courtesy of Engleberg Antiks. c.1940s-50s. $245-275

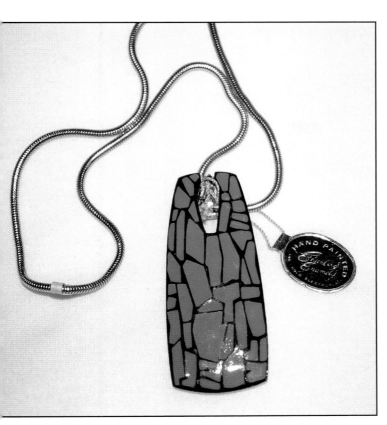

Three-inch long green enamel pendant with gold finish and original chain. Signed "Eisenberg". Notice it still has a paper tag and has probably never been worn. Courtesy of Engleberg Antiks c.1970s. $75-125

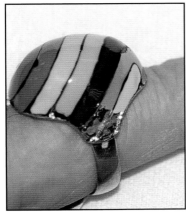

Multi-color dome shape enamel finish ring signed "Eisenberg". An unusual piece as not many signed Eisenberg rings are found. Courtesy of Engleberg Antiks. c.1970s. $75-100

A much newer signed Eisenberg Ice pendant with matching earrings. Large pink a. b. tear drop shape prong set rhinestones form the center of each piece and the remainder is covered with smaller similar stones. A nice set from the 1990s that is much lighter and not as high quality as the older Eisenberg. Authors' Collection. $75-100

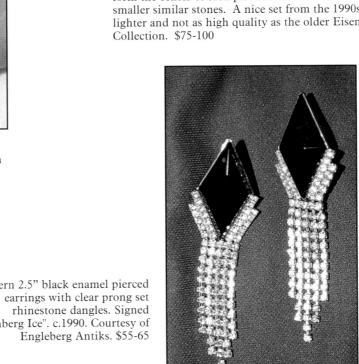

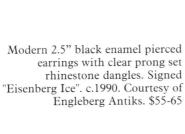

Modern 2.5" black enamel pierced earrings with clear prong set rhinestone dangles. Signed "Eisenberg Ice". c.1990. Courtesy of Engleberg Antiks. $55-65

If you compare an unsigned piece with a signed piece, and they are both of similar age, quality, and condition, we believe the signed piece will be more valuable. It is also quite possible that the signed piece will appreciate more in value than the unsigned one. Some designer's jewelry is more popular and more in demand than others, and two similar pieces with different designers' signatures will also vary in value, depending on the signature alone.

Our suggestion to a collector, or especially anyone who buys jewelry for resale, is to take the time to learn the designer's names, logos, and history. You will find added pleasure when you shop and will save or make money in the long run.

Two small 1.5 inch enamel bird pins. One is signed "Boucher" and the other bears only a number but is of very similar quality and appears to be an unsigned Boucher. Good example of a signature making a pin worth more than one without it. Can you tell which one is signed? Remember to turn jewelry over and look at the back. Courtesy of Engleberg Antiks. c.1950s. Unsigned $35-40 Signed $65-75.

Very nice 2.5" bow shape brooch signed "Eisenberg Original" and "Sterling". A very nice brooch with some larger clear prong set rhinestones and many pavé-set. It is a nice collectors' piece. Courtesy of Engleberg Antiks. c.1930s-40s. $375-450

Also very nice, but this near 3" bow brooch is unsigned and has a silver finish metal.. It has a variety of large, various shape, rhinestones, either prong or pavé-set. Brooch is very similar in age and condition to the signed bow but its value is lower, mostly because of the lack of a signature. Courtesy of Engleberg Antiks. c.1930s-40s. $75-125

Signed costume jewelry can be found dating well back into the 1800s, as the signed Norwegian set pictured on pages 16 and 17 demonstrates. Our experience in buying would lead us to believe that the general practice of the application of signatures to costume jewelry started in the 1930s and was common after 1940. Some designers of fine costume jewelry are still not applying their name to the jewelry today. Look at the quality of the following examples of unsigned jewelry manufactured after signing became popular.

This is a large over 3" unsigned brooch composed of clear prong set rhinestones on different layers of silver metal. It has four rhinestone covered dangles that end with larger tear drop stones. Courtesy of Engleberg Antiks. c.1950s-60s. $115-130

Elegance in an unsigned necklace. It is 24" of clear rhinestones with multiple 4" danglers. Silver metal. Several round balls, covered with rhinestones, provides great accents. Courtesy of Engleberg Antiks. c.1960s. $175-225

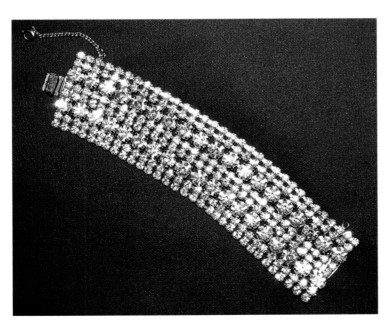

All prong set clear rhinestones bring elegance to this unsigned 7" bracelet that is over 3" wide. Courtesy of Engleberg Antiks. c.1960s. $105-125

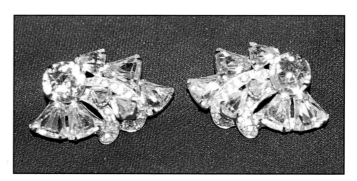

Quality 1.5" unsigned multi-layer clip earrings with clear rhinestones on silver metal. Courtesy of Engleberg Antiks. c.1950s. $25-30

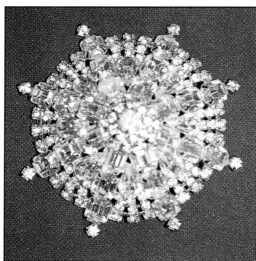

This quality 3.25" brooch features multiple size clear rhinestones, prong set, in a circular pattern. Courtesy of Engleberg Antiks. c.1960s. $65-85

Very eye-catching, 3.5", dangling type, clip earrings with clear rhinestones on silver metal. Courtesy of Engleberg Antiks. c.1970s. $45-55

Multi-level, baguette shape, clear rhinestones are used on these lovely 2" unsigned clip earrings. Silver metal. Courtesy of Engleberg Antiks. c.1950s. $45-55

A musician's dream. Clarinet, trumpet, and guitar combined with the player's hands and dangling musical notes all with heavy gold finish form this 3.5" pin. Authors' Collection. c.1970s. $45-55

Four flowers with large pastel rhinestone centers and clear pavé-set rhinestones cover the petals, heavy gold leaves for a background, make this a striking 5" unsigned piece. Authors' Collection. c.1940s. $145-175

Unsigned sterling brooch, with very heavy metal and gold wash, has a wonderful south of the border influence. Matching sombrero earrings have colorful enamel highlights. Set shown as signed in some books. Authors' Collection. c.1940s. $175-250

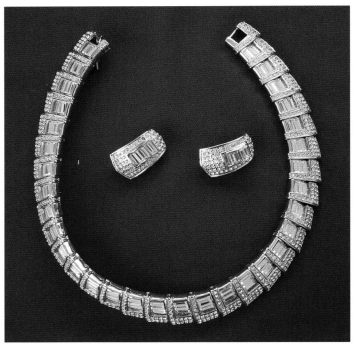

Newer 18" exceptional quality necklace in gold finish metal with matching spring, screw back earrings. Authors' Collection. c.1970s. $225-275

Newer 16", extremely well constructed, necklace with heavy silver finish and lots of clear round and baguette rhinestones. Matching earrings. Authors' Collection. c.1970s. $225-275

Close up shows the heavy gold finish, nice faux pearls and dozens of pavé-set clear rhinestones in this finely designed set.

If the signature was not applied to most costume jewelry prior to the 1940s, you may wonder how you identify jewelry from that period. The designs of the pieces seemed to change greatly around that time. Dress clips and fur clips became less practical and were replaced with pin backs. The lovely old Victorian styles were replaced and a new era seemed to begin. Note the differences in styles between the signed pieces in this section and the following older, unsigned pieces.

Nice shell cameo of lady in low cut dress. Metal is 900 silver (not quite sterling) and is made to wear as either a pin or pendant. c.1880-1900. Authors' Collection. $225-300

Very nice 2" shell cameo features the "Three Graces". Sterling silver with a gold wash, made to be worn as either a pin or pendant. c.1860 Authors' Collection. $350-450

A 2" hand carved shell cameo set in sterling with a carving of a lady in a high collared dress with flowers. Notice the detail on this item that may be worn as pin or pendant. c.1910. Authors' collection. $225-300

Delicate leaf design adorns the sides of this beautiful Victorian cameo ring. Rolled gold c.1860-1880 Authors' Collection. $175-200

The face of the ring is striking with the white face over black faux jet. Authors' Collection.

A large emerald cut onyx stone highlights this vintage, one size fits all, ring. Tiny leaves curling up the sides make it unique. Authors' collection. $75-100

Sterling chain and dainty clear faceted crystals compose this delicate necklace. c. early 1900s. Authors' Collection. $75-100

Sterling chain and dainty clear faceted crystals with a tear drop center stone. Authors' Collection. c.early 1900s. $75-100

This is a very unique necklace with sterling chain and round pale blue flat glass stones reverse carved, (intaglio) with a dainty rose pattern. Wonderful detail. Authors' collection. c.1920s. $125-200

Sterling chain and more dainty clear crystals makes this the nicest of the three delicate necklaces shown. Authors' Collection. c.early 1900s.$125-175

Four old bar pins from 2" to over 3" in length all with a gold finish and delicate designs. Authors' Collection. c.early 1900s. Each $65-85

Open-back amethyst stones make this delicate sterling, over 3", bar pin a real eye-catcher. Authors' Collection. c.1920s. $150-165

Two lapel pins and eight 2" to 3" stick pins: Larger lapel pin has a nice engraving in the gold finish and a white glass stone with touches of pink. The smaller lapel pin has a delicate grape vine design. The stick pins, left to right, square cut citrine on gold finish metal with a scallop design; tiny bee and gold finish; oval amethyst cabochon and gold finish; grape cluster of tiny pearls; Tested 14k gold with opal and ruby; oval goldstone and gold finish; Tested 14k gold with engraved design; four sapphires on tested 14k gold. Authors' Collection. $35-200 each

Three very old and unique pins all with large open back stones. See the delicate work in the metal on all three. The lower pin has an amber colored center stone with tiny pink rhinestones at the edge. We would question if the stones in this piece are original. Courtesy of Engleberg Antiks. c.early 1900s.$45-125

Three large bird pins all the same size and age but with different stones. Each is unique in its own way. Courtesy of Engleberg Anitks. C.1940s. Each $95-145

A long 24" brass chain with very detail pattern adds beauty to this Czech pendant with large amethyst baguette stone and enamel. Authors' Collection. c.1910-20. $125-150

Four old pins each with a large open back center stone and detail metal work. Courtesy of Engleberg Antiks. Early 1900s.$35-95 each

Long 24 inch Bohemian glass necklace with six 4 inch dangling strands of tiny beads. Matching earrings. Authors Collection. c.1920s. $100-150

Brass chain with a large topaz center stone and multiple strands of small topaz beads dangling make this a very attractive Czech. necklace. Authors' Collection. c.1910-20. $75-125

Close up of Czech pendant shows tiny enamel flowers and intricate metal work. Authors' Collection. $95-125

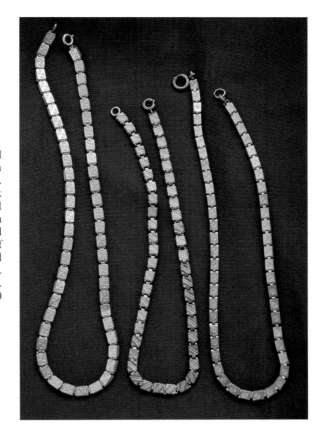

Three 14" to 16" rolled gold bookchain necklaces. c.1860-1880. Notice each link resembles a small book. Each side has a different design. Rolled gold was thin layers of gold rolled and layered over other metals. Authors' Collection. Each $125-150

Two lovely old bracelets. One is a gold slider with delicate gold leaves and flowers around a carved shell cameo. The other is a long gold bracelet with an amethyst cabochon stone. Authors' Collection. Cameo $265-Amathest $175

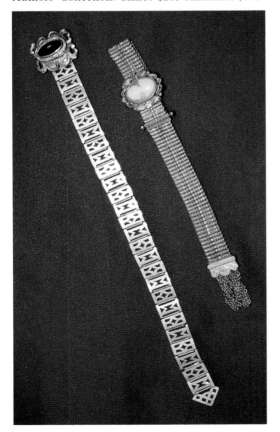

Rolled gold bookchain necklace with cameo clasp. c. 1880s. Authors' Collection. $175-250

How Much is It Worth?

There are several factors that determine the value of a piece of costume jewelry. Naturally, the physical attributes of the piece are a big factor. For example, large brooches are usually more valuable and collectable than small ones. Condition follows a close second. Other factors are the age, how rare the piece is, and who designed it. These all must be considered, but in the end, it will probably be how badly you want it for your collection that counts.

Remember, if you are a collector, you have a different perspective than a dealer buying for resale who must purchase the jewelry at a price that will allow them to make a profit. Many dealers use half of the retail value as a measure. It does not matter if you are a collector or a dealer, you should both have the same starting place. The first thing you need to determine is its retail value.

Experience and knowledge are the only things that will assure that you don't overpay for a piece of jewelry. Repeat buying from a dealer you know and trust can also help lower your cost and help you avoid overpaying. To gain knowledge we suggest you do the following:

Go to antique shows and pay particular attention to the prices of the pieces you are interested in collecting. Ask the dealer what your discount would be if you bought certain pieces and then ask them what it would be if you purchase several items. Dealers always ask what the "dealer discount" is. They usually get better discounts because they are repeat buyers and will usually buy more than one item.

You should go to antique shops. Try ones that have jewelry dealers who have large inventories and look at prices on pieces similar to those at the show. Ask the sales person about discounts. Almost all dealers will allow discounts but they will not usually be as good as the ones they will allow at shows.

Purchase several costume jewelry books, as each will usually have 300 to 400 photos in them along with a price guide. The prices here may be higher or lower than they are in your geographic area, depending on where the book's author lives. You should probably allow yourself some discount, when figuring the value, to make the prices comparable with the ones at shows and shops.

If you have a computer, search for jewelry auctions and look up the type of jewelry you are interested in. These sales prices may also vary from the local show and store prices, because the bidders come from all parts of the world.

If you compare the information you have gathered, from the sources listed, you will be able to determine the approximate price range of the pieces you are interested in. Be sure you are comparing pieces in similar condition. Flea market, garage sale, estate sale and local auction sale prices should not be used to determine actual values. Most of the time, the people who sell this way have distorted ideas of the value of the jewelry and will either almost give it away or price it at "diamond" prices. Auctions have such a variety of people who attend, the jewelry will seldom sell for its actual value.

There is one last thing to note in determining the value of costume jewelry. If the item is in the original box or case, it is usually worth more. This is especially true with very old jewelry. Note the original case from the 1800s, in which the David Anderson set rests, is shown in the first section.

After your review and comparison of similar items, you should have a better idea of what certain types of jewelry are worth. You are ready to shop.

Knowing what costume jewelry is worth and being able to recognize it is very essential but can sometimes be painful. On numerous occasions, people have proudly shown us the Christmas tree wall plaques or other items they have created with costume jewelry. As you look carefully at these you will often recognize designer pieces worth hundreds of dollars glued to a piece of plywood, ruined forever. You cringe and bite your lip.

Just a reminder to keep jewelry in its original box, whenever possible.

The Rhinestones

Regardless of whether you are a collector or a dealer, you want to be certain that you know the item you are purchasing is in good condition, or that its problems are limited to those you know how to correct. We do not want to take the fun out of purchasing costume jewelry by making it complicated. This section, and the two that follow, are designed to help you know how to detect problems. If you find a piece of jewelry with the problems we are pointing out, it does not necessarily mean you should not purchase the piece. That will depend on your ability to correct the problem and your desire to spend the effort it takes. It will, however, reduce the value and should improve your chances to negotiate a lower price.

First, make sure there are no stones missing. It is usually the missing smaller pavé-set stones that are harder to detect. Look very carefully. We have been buying for a long time and still occasionally miss this.

Look carefully at the stones to be sure they are all clear. If closed back stones have gotten damp, the foil on the back may be damaged and they will loose their reflective qualities and appear dark. In the case of open back stones, with foil backing, part of the foil may have been worn off and these will not reflect correctly and you will be able to see through the stone where the foil is missing.

Lovely 4.5" pin, unsigned, spray. The tips of the petals are covered with clear pavé-set rhinestones, but one is missing. This is an easy stone to match and replace. Larger red stones are open back but are not prong set, as they normally would be, but are glued in place. Not worth much even if you replace the stone. Authors' Collection. c.1950s. $45-55

Oriental look in this unsigned 15" necklace with faces, green stones, and tiny faux pearls. Matching clip earrings. Notice the missing stones and damaged pearls. Would you buy it this way? Authors' Collection. Set including bracelet in repaired condition $175-200

If you turn this piece over, you will be able to see where the foil is worn. If all of the stones on a piece are slightly darkened this may just be due to age. In that case, you alone can determine if the piece is worth saving. Open back stones that do not have foil backing will not have this problem.

Check the larger stones carefully to be certain that they do not have cracks or chips, either of which would have been caused from being dropped or bumped. Remember, the stones are glass and must be handled with care. Look closely at the stones and then run a finger over the edges to detect chips.

Matching 7" oriental looking bracelet.

Look to be sure that someone has not replaced stones and has done it incorrectly. Make sure the stones fit the holes the designer planned for them. If stones were replaced with larger ones they will stick up slightly or if smaller, they will be lower than the others. The second replacement error is to try to fill up the hole left by a missing stone with one of a different shape. Third, you need to hold the piece out and look to see if all of the stones are the same color. At the same time, look at the stones to see if one or more stand out because they are cut differently from the others and do not have the same number of facets. If poorly cut stones are mixed with diamond cut stones, they will stand out.

Heart shaped, unsigned pin with various prong set rhinestones. Good example of open backed stones with foil. About 1.75". Courtesy of Engleberg Antiks. $30-35

Occasionally a piece that appears to have rhinestones in it will have plastic stones. If you are in doubt at all, tap one of the stones against a tooth, or tap it gently with a key, and you will be able to tell by the sound if it is glass or plastic. Plastic stones will greatly reduce the value of a piece.

If you find something you like, and it has one of the problems noted above, a question arises. Do you purchase it and try to replace the stones that are bad? If you are a dealer, you must learn how to replace stones correctly or you will miss many good buys. A collector, however, can be more particular and if they wish, never learn to replace stones. They will pass up some good buys if they don't. The objective of examining jewelry so closely before buying it is to be sure you don't buy something that cannot be repaired. If you do buy it, make sure that the price reflects the condition of the piece. Several years ago we bought a bird pin at a very good price, as it was rare, but we still have not found a replacement stone.

Back of heart shaped pin. Notice the open back stones that have foil backs. These must be checked for wear before buying.

Rules for purchasing jewelry with missing or bad stones

If you don't have extraordinary skills at replacing stones, we suggest that you do not purchase a piece with bad or missing stones, if it does not meet the following rules. Remember, replacing a stone correctly requires that you have a stone the same size, shape, color and cut as the original. This applies whether you replace the stone yourself or have someone else do it.

Missing or damaged pavé-set rhinestones

If a pavé-set stone is missing and you know you have, or can obtain, a correct stone, you should be able to replace it. You can buy the piece and replace the stone, but ask for a discount. If, however, a pavé-set stone has turned dark, and is still in place, you may or may not ever be able to remove it so it can be replaced. We even resorted to a drill to remove smaller stones and, at times, were unsuccessful. *We would not recommend buying costume jewelry if any of the smaller pavé-set stones are dark.* If only one or two larger pavé-set stones are bad, you will probably be able to remove them and may consider purchasing the item. If you do replace a pavé-set stone, remember to use glue designed for models and hobbies, and not one of the new powerful ones. They are too strong and may damage the foil; you will have a dark stone again within a short time.

Missing or damaged prong set rhinestones

If a prong set stone is missing or bad in any way, and you have, or can obtain an exact match, you may be able to replace it. If, however, you break off any of the prongs the remaining prongs may hold the stone but you certainly are not returning the piece to its original condition. If only one or two prong set stones need replacing you may want to gamble a little and purchase the piece. If, however, several prong set stones need replacing you should pass up this purchase.

As with the case of our missing stone in the bird pin, shown previously, watching, and hunting for the replacement stone to repair a rare, expensive piece, can be an adventure in itself. In any case, if you purchase a piece with one or more bad stones, be sure it is reflected in the price you pay.

This is a rare signed 3.5" Reinad Brooch that we could not resist. It has one large, very difficult to match, stone missing from a wing. We paid very little for it, but enjoy looking for a replacement stone. Sometimes you may want to gamble like this. Authors' Collection. c.1930s. Restored $1,000-1,200

Metals and Finishes

Whether a piece of costume jewelry you are considering has rhinestones or not, you should examine the metal, or other construction material, and the finish to be certain it is in original, or at least acceptable condition. Wear or aging will affect the metal on a piece of jewelry, but may only add character and may make it more valuable. Damage or excessive wear may make it worthless. The following items must be checked before buying.

Check everything to be sure its mechanical parts work.

Make sure that all of the moving parts work, and work correctly. Fasten and unfasten all clasps. Open and close hinged parts, especially bracelets, to be certain they will close and will hold tightly. Check the earrings to be sure that the clips, screw backs, or posts will hold them securely. Stretch expansion bracelets slightly.

Check for missing pieces

Look carefully at the design to see if it appears to have all of the leaves, flowers, or what ever parts it should have. If it appears questionable, look to see if there are any bare ends where the metal has broken off. Look especially close at complicated and delicate designs constructed with rhinestones, pearls, and small findings, as in the case of signed Haskell pieces, as they are often constructed with fine wire and parts may be missing.

Look for signs of repair

Look for signs that indicate a repair. Dried glue on the back of a piece will be evidence of a repair to the metal. A solder repair may show up as a rough spot or lump but, in any case, will usually be a different color than the original finish. You can almost be certain that the piece was broken in some way if dried glue or solder is found. If you notice either, find out why, before buying it. The example showed tiny signs of repair, but it was such a fine piece we bought it anyway. Buying it was a mistake. Look at it as it should be, and as it is with part broken off.

This 4" long signed Mazer brooch was too beautiful and inexpensive for us not to gamble. It had a solder mark on a spot on the back. Although it is a quality piece, and is beautiful as shown, it soon broke. The following slide shows how it looks now. Authors' Collection.

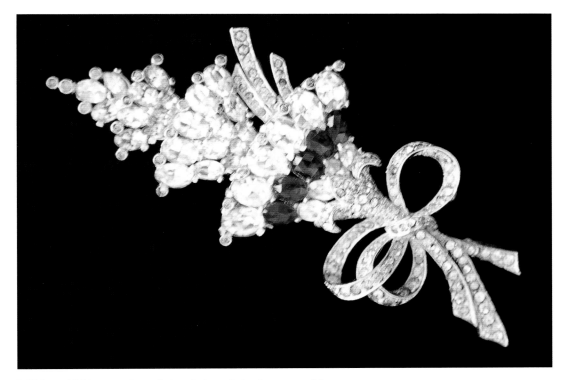

Still beautiful but one branch is missing. It is almost worthless.

Look for alterations

Look for signs of alterations to the original design. It is not unusual for someone to alter an old dress or fur clip. They will usually remove the original fastener and replace it with a pin back. If you are buying large old pieces, from the 1930s and 1940s, and they are pins, look closely for signs that they may have been altered.

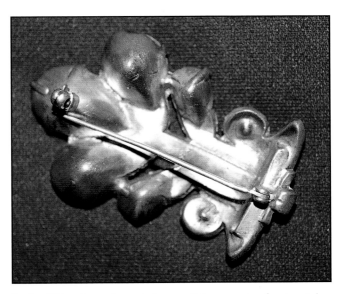

Back of Eisenberg shows it is one of those made of pot metal. It is signed "Eisenberg Original" as expected, but it has been altered. This was originally a fur clip, but has been converted to a pin. Nice to wear, but is not in original condition. If in original condition, it would be worth $250-275

A beautiful Eisenberg Original brooch which appears to be in near perfect condition with large clear prong set rhinestones. Courtesy of Engleberg Antiks. c.1930s. $100-125.

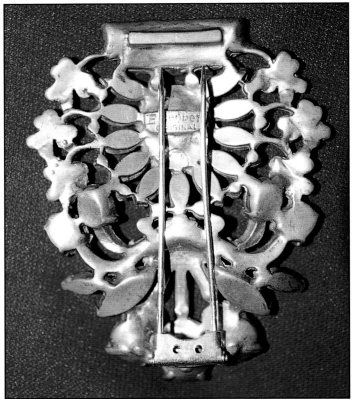

Beautiful fur clip, over 4" long with large clear prong set rhinestones of different sizes. Signed "Eisenberg Original". Courtesy of Engleberg Antiks. A gorgeous piece to wear and in excellent condition on the front. c.1930s. As is $250-300

Back of fur clip. Note, the clip has been moved from one end of the piece to the other. Why someone would do this is a mystery but note, it is not in original condition and if not altered would be worth $700-750

Examine the metal finish

This applies to all costume jewelry. If it has scratches or other marks in the metal, we suggest you avoid it. The scratches will always be there. If it is an enamel piece, it is almost impossible to repair the enamel finish and bring it back to original condition. Avoid enamel pieces that someone else has tried to refinish. These are worth little or nothing.

No matter what metal a piece of costume jewelry is made of, it is usually covered by a thin layer of silver or gold. This finish is made to wear for years and may never wear off, but you need to examine it when you are considering buying. If it is worn off evenly and the appearance is still appealing, it may be acceptable.

If it has worn unevenly on the front, it is questionable. If it does not have any stones, it can be refinished with the proper equipment. We had a few pieces refinished and our jeweler only charged us five to ten dollars to refinish each piece and made them look like new. We do not, however, think you can normally have a rhinestone piece successfully refinished without removing the stones. Most refinishing processes require heat and it will crack or loosen the stones.

Examine faux pearl finish

If you are purchasing a piece that has faux pearls, be certain they do not have any chips out of the finish or are not peeling. Faux pearls have a thin coating that will last for years but they may become damaged. Hold the pearls in the light and look closely for rough spots or small spots that are a different color than the other pearls. Look between the pearls. Chipped and peeled spots will only get bigger. You may replace a pearl but it will mean restringing. Finding a replacement pearl the exact color may also be a problem.

Know what beads are made of

If you are buying beads, remember that plastic beads are not usually worth much, unless they are Bakelite. Tap a bead against one of your teeth and you will know if it is glass. If you don't want to do that, just remember, glass is cold to touch and plastic is warm. Be sure the strand is strung tightly, if you do not want to restring it. Better quality beads are usually knotted between each bead.

We are not going to tell you not to buy a piece of jewelry that has one of the problems listed above. As dealers, we would not purchase for resale any jewelry that was broken or had been repaired or altered. If you are a collector, you might like the piece so well you want it for your collection anyway. If you are a dealer the price might be so good you think you can repair it or make money selling it "as is." In any case, you should certainly be able to purchase the piece at a very good price. Just be certain that you have considered the items we have pointed out.

Large 4" signed Eisenberg Original. This sterling bow is a good example of a large open back prong set stone. The pale blue stone is perfect. It originally was a wonderful piece but note the large amount of uneven wear on the front. Still wearable but it does have excess wear. Courtesy of Engleberg Antiks. c.1940s. As is $125-175

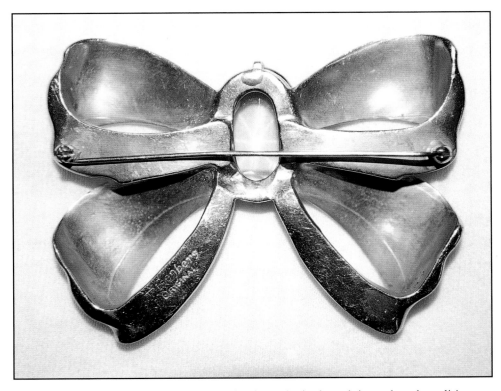

This is the back of the large Eisenberg sterling bow. A nice brooch in unaltered condition but it has excess wear on front and back. Could be refinished but center stone might need to be removed. If refinished value would be $700-750.

Things to Consider

At this point, you have checked condition of the stones, the metal, and the finish on the piece you are considering to purchase. What else could possibly be wrong with it? You should consider the following before buying, whether for your collection or for resale. It will affect the price you pay, and the eventual value.

Does the jewelry fit?

Fit is very important and the buyer will usually consider it. We would not feel right to not mention it. A dealer may overlook this because they do not intend to wear it. A bracelet should go around your wrist snuggly but with a little space to move. Seven inches is the usual length of a bracelet. A choker must be long enough to go around the neck comfortably. A necklace, or pendant, must be long enough to hang, as it was designed. If part of the strand has broken off, and someone moved the clasp, it will fasten correctly but will be too short. If you love the necklace, but it is too short, remember, you may be able to purchase an extender. An extender is a three to six inch piece of chain, or rhinestones, with a hook clasp on each end. They come in either gold or silver and may be purchased many places where new costume jewelry is sold.

Is it a "set" or a "marriage"?

Is the set actually a set, or is it pieces that someone has put together? Look at the color of the metal. Do all pieces have the same color metal finish? Sometimes one piece of a set may have been worn more often than the other. The finish on that piece may be more worn. Do all of the pieces have the same design, shape and color stones? Often someone will put earrings, necklaces, bracelets or pins together to complete a set because it is more valuable than the pieces are separately. They may look alike at first glance, but are not actually a set. Putting unmatched pieces together to make a set is often referred to as a "marriage." You may love the set and not really care if it is a perfect match, but remember, it is worth less if you ever want to sell it to a more discerning buyer.

Purple rhinestones, gold metal , and design all match in this signed Hollycraft brooch and earrings, dated 1950. Hollycraft was one of the few companies that dated its jewelry, so the date can also be used in the comparison to see if pieces are actually a set. This is definitely a set. Authors' Collection. $95-145

Clear and purple marquise and round prong set rhinestones are used primarily in this signed Eisenberg. Clear pavé-set rhinestones are used on the dainty curved overlays. Notice the same shape and color stones are used in the earrings. The stones are also set using the same method. The metal is silver on necklace and earrings. This definitely is a set. Authors' Collection. c.1940. $325-450

This you can easily see is a "marriage". The Eisenberg signature on the bracelet is from the 1940s while the earrings are pierced and signed Eisenberg Ice. They both have very nice round diamond cut clear rhinestones on silver metal. Authors' Collection. Earrings $55-65 Bracelet $150-200

Is the signature correct?

Just because a piece has a name on it does not mean that it was made by that designer. It is relatively easy to change the clasp on a bracelet or necklace, or even the clips on a pair of earrings. If that is where the signature appears, the piece may not be what it appears to be. If the clasp is not the same metal finish as the main part of the jewelry, it may indicate that it was changed. Other than that, it is up to you. If you are buying signed jewelry you should study the style of the designer and, eventually, you will be able to tell if the signature is appropriate. If you are a collector, and restrict your buying to one designer, you will eventually become an expert and will know more than most dealers do about that designer's work.

Is it a reproduction?

This is not always a negative thing but you should be knowledgeable, and know that pieces are reproduced. When a jewelry company first designs a piece, they obtain a patent so others cannot legally copy it during the life of the patent. Sometimes, later in the life of the patent, or even after it ends, the same company will decide to reproduce it or another very similar in design. These usually bare the name of the originating company and are authentic. As an example, in the 1990s the Eisenberg Co. produced several brooches replicating the design of older Eisenberg pieces. They were produced using high quality stones and metal which may have even been better quality than the originals. Referred to as "Eisenberg Classics", they bear the Eisenberg Ice signature, and are dated. A certificate of authenticity accompanies each piece. These are, in our opinion, very good buys and will increase in value.

This signed "DeNicola" necklace has large purple cabochons prong set in silver metal. Matched with Jomaz earrings it makes a stunning set. When worn together the difference in the shades of purple does not show up as it does in the picture. The difference in the color of the stones, even without the different signatures, should convince you it is a "marriage". Authors' Collection. Earrings $50 Necklace c.1950s. $375-425

Sometimes a piece of jewelry is reproduced by a company other than the one that held the original patent. Companies will sometimes even apply another company's name to jewelry that company never made. This is difficult for us to believe as the pieces are often of such good quality and design we cannot understand why the manufacturer did not apply their own name. The pieces originally sell for very reasonable prices, but as they pass through future sales, the prices increase and they are often priced as though they were authentic old designer pieces. Only experience and knowledge of the designers work will protect you from this. If you like a piece and want it for a collection, buy it. If you are a collector, or a dealer, you should realize that it is not worth as much as it would be if authentic. When you sell it someday, your return on the sale will be lower. A costume jewelry dealer should not sell these to you without disclosing their origin, if they have any idea they are not authentic. We have enclosed a few examples of pieces we bought as new, that we believe fall into this category.

The metal on this fine brooch is plated with rhodium. It has fine prong set rhinestones. This piece signed "Eisenberg Ice 94" is one of a series of replications of older brooches by Eisenberg called "classics". When it was sold it came with a certificate of authenticity. It is very collectible and the value will increase with time. Authors' Collection. $225-275

Over 3" long and signed "Coro Craft" this is a fine piece. Engravings on top and around the edge of the shell are wonderful. It has a nice gold wash on the metal and has a circle of pavé-set rhinestones on the shell. We liked it and purchased it new in the 1990s but know is has to be a reproduction. Author's Collection. $95-125

This lovely swan brooch signed "Coro Craft" features unusual shaped and textured stones on the wings. It has a very nice gold finish. This was also purchased new in the 1990s and is a reproduction. If old and authentic it would be worth several hundred dollars. Authors' Collection. $95-125

This is called a "jelly belly". It is defined by the clear Lucite body. It is a sterling fly brooch with a very nice gold finish. It was purchased new in the 1990s and is a reproduction of much older pieces of this type. It is worth less than $100, while authentic older signed ones sell for $400 and up. Authors' Collection.

Where To
Get the Best Buys?

It is important that you know where and how to get the best buys. If you are a collector, it will mean that you can purchase more pieces for your collection. If you are a dealer, it will mean that you will have a larger profit when you resale the item. We have tried to provide a listing of the places and methods that will give you the most for your money. Some will not be practical for you, as you may not have the time or patience they require.

The importance of knowing where to buy is best illustrated by a true story. We stopped by an estate sale late in the first day of the sale. They had a very nice Schiaparelli set for sale for $250. We looked at it but did not happen to be in the mood to buy as we were on our way to the beach. The following morning we were returning and we stopped at the sale again. The set was now $125 and a terrific bargain. We bought it. The following Friday we were working at an antique show. We immediately sold the set to another dealer for $300. Later in the day, we saw the set in a third dealer's booth. The price was now $900. Think about the events. The set was available for purchase four different times. Where do you want to be in the purchase chain?

Bulk purchases

The best buys we made as dealers would not usually be practical for the collector. These were the few occasions when we were able to purchase all of the jewelry an individual owned. It might be a dealer going out of business, an estate, or just someone who was tired of collecting. In cases like this, we ask the seller to name the price. In this way we can avoid insulting the seller buy offering too little. We can accept their offer, make a counter offer, or reject it. No matter which way it goes, everyone is happy. We turned down an offer to purchase a dealers entire inventory, at a show, for $2,500. It came to less than $2 per piece. It was all unsigned and was not the quality we usually handled or we would have bought it. Using hindsight, we should have bought it anyway. Someone else did and probably made a nice profit. If you get a chance to purchase a bulk lot, and you are careful, you can end up with the best individual piece prices you will ever get.

You usually do not have a lot of time to make the decision. You must make the calculations in your head or possibly on a piece of scratch paper. We suggest you roughly count the good pieces, figure out how much they would be per item by dividing the number of pieces into the offered price. You will be fairly certain if it is a deal you want. Our last bulk purchase was from an individual who would not name a price. The batch included several gold pieces with stones, all of which turned out to be diamonds (we did not know until later when we tested them) which we usually did not sell, 40 stick pins, a couple of cameos and several pieces of costume jewelry of which one piece was signed. Applying various prices to the different types Dave made an offer of $900 (Lee about fainted). Was it a gamble, or not? The offer was based on $150 each for gold pieces, $5 stick pins, $50 cameos, and $25 each for costume jewelry. We found out at the next show when the gold pieces sold for over $1000 each.

Flea markets and garage sales

The best single purchases are made at flea markets and garage sales. You will undoubtedly find some costume jewelry bargains at these places. The buyers are usually selling items they no longer wear, something they inherited and don't especially like, or they are a dealer who is satisfied with a minimum profit. They usually will not know the true value. The drawback is, you will have to hunt, hunt, and hunt. Quality pieces of costume jewelry that are clean and in good condition are few and far between. If you have the time and enjoy going to flea markets and garage sales you will occasionally be rewarded. In this same category are the resale clothing stores and used merchandise stores operated by charitable organizations. The only problem with the latter is that they usually have a volunteer working for them who prices the jewelry and then purchases it at the bargain price. When you go shopping, always carry your loupe', as you never know what you will find.

Examples of pieces of some gold and gemstones we found at garage sales, while we were looking for costume jewelry, are shown.

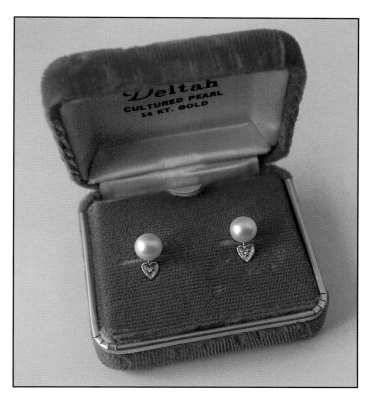

Beautiful 14k white gold, pierced earrings with a large cultured pearl and tiny diamond. Purchased at an estate sale for $2. Authors' Collection. $125-175

Detailed engraving and ruby can be seen in this close up of an Aztec looking 14k gold bracelet. Purchased at second day of garage sale for $10. Authors' Collection. $250-275

A signed DeNicola goat brooch purchased at a flea market. Authors' Collection. c.1960s. $75-95

Aztec looking design in this 1.25" pendant of 18k gold on a 14k gold chain. The stone on the pendant is an emerald. Bought the second day of a garage sale for $10. Authors' Collection. $175-225

Estate sales

Estate sales will provide a better chance of finding some good costume jewelry than flea markets or garage sales. Relatives, however, tend to take the good pieces. In order to get in first you need to be there early but not too many people are willing to get up at four in the morning to wait for a sale to open. These sales tend to be two days long and you may get some real bargains by being there at opening time on the second day when prices are cut in half.

Necklace is 15" signed "Hollycraft Corp 1957" and is shown with matching 1.5" earrings. Dainty blue flowers with rhinestone centers and baguette highlights make this an unusual piece. Found the second day at an estate sale. Authors' Collection. $175-225

This 4.5" leaf pin with green and brown enamel on gold plated metal to give it an autumn look is signed "Weiss". Set is complete with matching clip earrings. Purchased at a flea market. Authors' Collection. c.1950s. $75-85

This signed Haskell is our reminder to ourselves not to over bid for an item on the on-line auctions. It is very new and is mostly a metal chain. Authors' Collection. c.1990s. $55-65

On-line auctions

On-line auctions may rate next for bargains. These certainly provide the buyer with a large number of pieces to choose from with the least amount of effort. This market probably fluctuates more with the economy then others. We have gotten a few real bargains buying on-line but we did not buy that way for long. You only see a picture of the jewelry before you bid and must rely on whatever information the seller provides. I sent many pieces back because they were not designed by the company the seller thought they were or because they were not in good condition. If you buy a piece of costume jewelry on-line and are happy with the transaction, watch for that dealer's merchandise and bid on it when they offer something you want. You can always bid low on items that do not have a reserve. Occasionally you will get a bargain.

We keep a Haskell necklace, that we purchased on-line, in our inventory as a reminder of what happens when you are not careful. It was offered as a Haskell and actually was as represented so we did not return it. It had a wonderful picture and we (Dave) really overpaid for it. You could not tell from the picture its age or how poorly it was constructed. We will show it to you but are ashamed to tell you what we paid.

Local auctions

Local auctions probably rate next for costume jewelry bargains. If you have a good knowledge of the value of costume jewelry you can get some real buys. This is certainly one place where collectors have the advantage over dealers when the jewelry is sold by the piece. They can bid any amount up to the true value of the piece while the dealer must stop with a lower bid that leaves a margin for profit. The collector will lose the advantage if the whole lot of jewelry is sold together. Usually collectors don't want to buy a lot of pieces they have no use for. If you plan to buy at an auction, preview the sale and look carefully at the pieces in advance. Decide how much you are willing to pay so you will not bid more than the item is worth. If you don't do this, you may get caught up in the excitement of the sale and will overpay. When you are ready to bid, get close enough so you can see the item being sold and be certain someone has not stolen the piece you wanted, or moved it to a different tray so they can buy one tray and get all of the good pieces. (It Happens.) Estate auctions are by far the best.

Nice unsigned 16" necklace with heavy gold plate and nice clear baguette highlights. Authors' Collection. c.1960. $55-65

Antiques shows

Antiques shows are a better place to look for bargains than any of those previously mentioned, for the amount of time invested. If you cruise the shows looking for the dealer who has small amounts of jewelry and find a piece that you want, you will usually get a bargain. If they sell all kinds of antiques they are not usually very knowledgeable in the field of costume jewelry and they will often give you really good prices. Finding the good piece in these booths will be the problem. If, however, you stop at the jewelry booths, you will find a real variety of pieces, usually clean and in good condition, and perhaps the exact piece for your collection. The price may be a little more than you want to pay but remember that in order to get the piece, the dealer spent the time it took to find it. They also must absorb all of the cost of attending the show. If you find a dealer you like and they have jewelry you can use, become a repeat buyer and they will give you their best prices. They will start saving pieces for you and may occasionally buy a piece specifically with you in mind. This is true whether you are a collector or a dealer. Discounts allowed at antique shows are usually greater than at antique shops. Always ask for the "best price."

Christmas tree pin, with a missing stone, was found at an antique mall for $2. Tree is signed Art. Authors' Collection. c.1950s. $25-35

This is a quality bracelet with two rows of clear, diamond cut rhinestones and safety chain in silver metal. Signed Eisenberg Ice. Courtesy of Engleberg Antiks. c.1960s. $135-175

Antiques malls

The antiques malls will often give you a good variety to choose from and add to your collection. The best buys come in antique malls where you can cruise the halls and find the single piece in a non-jewelry dealer's booth. We have made some terrific buys when a dealer had just opened a booth for the first time. One time, when we were traveling, we stopped at an antique mall and one dealer was closing out. We purchased five gorgeous Eisenberg Original brooches for $100 each. Almost any dealer will give you a discount from the tag price. Another time we stopped at a mall and, as we entered, Lee spied six Bakelite bangle bracelets (gum drop style, bright colors with large round spots). We asked the sales person to call the owner of the booth to get a price if we bought all six. We got a bargain and the owner was happy. If an individual price is a little more than you want to pay, or you want to buy several pieces, do not hesitate to ask the sales person to check with the owner for a special discount. What do you have to lose? Be practical, however, and don't expect them to call about a $25 item.

The dealers, in malls, who specialize in jewelry, will usually provide you clean jewelry in good condition at fair prices. Again, if you become a repeat buyer or make multiple purchases you will get their best prices. We hate to do it ourselves, but we cannot over emphasize the value of asking for discounts.

Nearly 100 photos in this book were taken at a single antique mall. It only represents a fraction of the pieces available there. Many of the pieces are used as illustrations but the others are presented here to show you the opportunities that you have to add to your collection with a little easy antique mall shopping.

Clear, round, diamond cut rhinestones line the entire length of this 16" signed Eisenberg necklace. Wide dangling centerpiece is the focal point. Courtesy of Engleberg Antiks. c.1950s-60s. $175-225

A 2.5" signed Eisenberg pin with matching dangle type clip earrings. Courtesy of Engleberg Antiks. c.1950s. $125-150

Large over 3" signed Eisenberg brooch with matching dangle clip earrings. Clear prong and pavé-set rhinestones on silver metal with multi layer construction. Courtesy of Engleberg Antiks. c.1940s-50s $135-155

Smaller 2.5" signed Eisenberg pin with matching clip earrings. Nice clear prong and pavé-set rhinestones. Courtesy of Engleberg Antiks. c.1950s. $95-125

White enamel hinged cuff bracelet with blue and green highlights signed "Hobé". Courtesy of Engleberg Antiks. c.1960s. $55-65

Beautiful mix of blue and clear prong set rhinestones compose this 16" necklace with matching earrings signed Eisenberg. Courtesy of Engleberg Antiks. c.1950s. $200-250

Gold finish choker with an expensive look. Signed "Givenchy". Note the round loops completely finished with clear pavé-set rhinestones. Courtesy of Engleberg Antiks. c.1970s. $95-105

Gold, hinged cuff bracelet with small, clear pavé-set, and large green prong set rhinestones with large faux pearl centers. Nice attention to detail and styling. Signed Hobé. Courtesy of Engleberg Antiks. c.1950s. $125-175

Cute 1.5 inch pin. A gold finish bird nest with a pearl egg and bird purchased on top. Courtesy of Engleberg Antiks. Signed Hattie Carnegie. c.1950s-60s. $45-55

Pineapple shaped gold finish 1.5" pin signed Hattie Carnegie. Courtesy of Engleberg Antiks. c.1960s. $45-55

A Four strand glass bead bracelet with rhinestones shown with matching earrings. Signed Eugene. Courtesy of Enbleberg Antiks. 1940s-50s. $125-135

A 2.5" sterling brooch signed Rosenstein. Gold finish with portions of the flower japanned. Courtesy of Engleberg Antiks. c.1950s. $150-225

Very nice 5" gold finish brooch with a large amber-brown stone and signed Sarah Coventry. This designer's better pieces are becoming more valuable and collectible. Courtesy of Engleberg Antiks. c.1960s-70s. $55-65

Over 3" Wendy Gell figure of a lady is finished with a full length black enamel evening gown. Courtesy of Engleberg Antiks. c.1970s. $75-90

Extra heavy metal and thick gold finished with pearl highlights. Signed "Napier". Courtesy of Enbleberg Antiks. c.1950s-60s. $55-65

Nice set with green glass and white plastic beads with delicate design. Signed Hobé. Courtesy of Engleberg Antiks. c.1950s. $125-150

Sleek and over 3" this gold and silver finish panther brooch with clear rhinestone collar is striking. Courtesy of Engleberg Antiks. c.1980s. $65-75

This three-piece set, signed "Germany", has lovely lavender rhinestones throughout. Courtesy of Engleberg Antiks. c.1940s. $125-175

This lovely brooch and earring set has fine detail work in the gold finished metal and very detailed Victorian picture. Signed "Germany". Courtesy of Engleberg Antiks. c.1940s. $75-105

An unusual mix of baguette and round rhinestones are used in this unsigned set. This, combined with use of blue and clear rhinestones, makes it very attractive. Courtesy of Engleberg Antiks. c.1950s. $125-135

Black glass drops highlight this 16" unsigned necklace.
Courtesy of Engleberg Antiks. c.1950s. $75-125

Three unsigned link bracelets with silver metal and prong set rhinestones.
Courtesy of Engleberg Antiks. c.1950s-60s. $45-65 each

Brilliant clear rhinestones on silver finish metal make this 2" pin great to wear on any solid color fabric. Courtesy of Engleberg Antiks. c.1950s. $45-65

Antique jewelry stores

You will normally find the best assortment of clean costume jewelry in good condition in stores that specialize in that merchandise. If you really want a special item for your collection you may find it there. These stores, however, have the greatest overhead and their jewelry will usually bear higher prices. They too will usually offer discounts and love repeat buyers.

Wherever you decide to look for pieces to add to your collection, have fun. Carry your loupe and look carefully before you buy.

This is an older 3.5 inch brooch with large brown cinnabar stones and pave2†set marcasites. Courtesy of Engleberg Antiks. c.1940s. $125-155.

Collecting:
What to Choose?

This is probably the only section in the book devoted strictly to the collector rather than the dealer. We don't know that this section is necessary, as each of you can certainly decide what to collect without our help. We would just like to present some ideas that might help you make your decision.

First, we suggest that you spend some time looking at costume jewelry so you know what you like best. Next, you should decide how much money you can afford to spend. Although what you spend on your collection is an investment, it does require money to feed the habit if you are to have fun. The closer your jewelry budget and your choice match, the more fun you will have.

If, for instance, you decide to collect high-end signed pieces, you will probably need to plan on spending at least $100 to $500 on each purchase. If you really let your appetite go wild you could spend as much as $1,500 or more on one piece. Remember, this is costume jewelry.

You can, however, select something by type rather than signature. There are also less expensive signed pieces that are very collectable. Suggestions in this area might be Christmas tree pins or butterfly pins. One lady, who comes to the antique shows, has developed a notebook with the picture of every known Christmas tree in it. She marks the photos of the ones she has in her collection and searches for the others. You can have a lovely collection of these for under $100 each. If your budget allows, once in a while, you can exceed that amount and add a more expensive item.

Costume jewelry collecting is certainly not restricted to women. For years we had a customer who collected Weiss exclusively. He attended most of the shows in the northwest. It was years before we learned his name. We knew him only as "the Weiss man." We are hoping to, someday, see his massive collection. We would have included it in this book but were unable to contact him.

The bracelet of the Hobé set. This piece not signed.
Remember all pieces of a set are not always signed.
Compare the materials and design when purchasing sets.

Beautiful three-piece Hobé set with 1.5" clip earrings, 17" necklace with beads that dangle 2.5", and a 7" bracelet. All pieces composed of clear pink and black crystal beads. Courtesy of Engleberg Antiks. c.1950s. $275-375

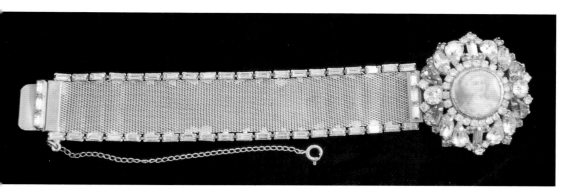

This 7" long gold finish early Hobé bracelet features a 1.5" portrait of a Victorian lady with multiple shape rhinestones surrounding it. Bracelet is 1" wide gold mesh. Authors' Collection. $450-525

Close-up of bracelet allows you to see the picture as well as the detail work surrounding it.

A gorgeous Schreiner 3" brooch. Reverse prong set champagne and green rhinestones on lower level. Long oval green stones and small dark pink ones surround a large pink, with white swirl, center stone on the top level. Authors' Collection. c.1960s. $425-550

Side view of Schreiner shows the depth of the brooch. This is a very typical Schreiner with the reverse rhinestones and depth of construction.

This is an elegant 4.5" signed Boucher brooch in near perfect condition. Blue, green, and pink cabochons look like "the real thing". Smaller red and clear rhinestones, all prong set, make this bird brooch a rainbow of color. Authors' Collection. c.1960s. $600-800

Large 3" gold butterfly pin with pearl highlights. Signed "Tortolani". Authors' Collection. $75-100

Great 2.25" signed Weiss butterfly pin in japanned metal and two shades of closed back blue rhinestones make this a striking piece. Owners' Collection. c.1950s-60s. $75-100

Almost a match. These are 1.5" and 2.5" multi-color prong set rhinestone Christmas tree pins signed "Eisenberg Ice". c. 1990s. Authors' Collection. Smaller $45-55 Larger $75-95

A signed Staret 4" butterfly brooch in wonderful condition. The large prong set multicolor rhinestones are foil backs. The smaller clear rhinestones are pavé set in gold metal. Usually when this piece is found, the foil on the stones has worn. All of the stones in this piece are mint. Very Rare. Authors' Collection. c.1930s. $1000-2000

Back of Weiss butterfly shows japanned metal.

An elegant 2.5" Christmas tree pin with brilliant prong set clear rhinestones. Signed "Eisenberg Ice". c. 1990s. Authors' Collection. $85-95.

A larger 3.25" signed Eisenberg Ice, Christmas tree pin with a multitude of green prong set elongated marquise shape rhinestones layered to give the tree depth. c.1990s. Authors' Collection. $95-105

Older two inch signed Art Christmas tree pin with frosted branches and a multitude of colored rhinestones as tree decorations. Authors' Collection. c.1950s. $65-75

If this is still too expensive, go down one more step and collect Christmas pins, less expensive tree pins or possibly jewelry depicting some type of "critters." These can be great fun and can be found for under $25.

Whatever you decide to collect, be sure to take into consideration our suggestions in the three sections on examining the pieces when you make a purchase. The following five items are a summary of our suggestions to you:

Collect something you can afford

If you overspend your personal budget, you will lose interest and will soon look at your collection as a liability. What will your significant other think when they find out how much you are spending?

Collect something you like

If you don't wear the jewelry in your collection, have it on display, or at least take it out and look at it or you will lose interest.

Buy only quality pieces

How to pick quality pieces that are in good condition is explained later in this book. If you are, however, fortunate enough to be skilled in the ability to repair jewelry, and are interested in doing it, you may make some terrific purchases for your collection.

Narrow your collection

Don't make your category so broad that you don't have to search to find new pieces. Searching is as much fun as buying.

Be knowledgeable

Last, learn everything you can about the type of jewelry you decide to collect. Knowing how old it is, who made it, and anything else about it, will bring you pleasure. With knowledge, you will make better choices.

Four inexpensive Christmas tree pins. None signed but they all have rhinestones tastefully placed on the tree as ornaments. Collectible and nice to wear. Courtesy of Engleberg Antiks. $15-35

Five inexpensive Christmas pins. The interesting design, color and materials incorporated in making these pieces make them unique. The top three have rhinestones and are metal while the two lower pins are plastic. Courtesy of Engleberg Antiks. $5 to $15.

Four inexpensive but collectible Christmas tree pins. None of these are signed or has many stones but they have decorative metal work which makes them attractive. Courtesy of Engleberg Antiks. $5-15

Four nice inexpensive Christmas pins. The wreath is signed "Art" and is the most expensive of the four. It is larger and has nice rhinestone decorations. The other three are unsigned but colorful and have good workmanship. Courtesy of Engleberg Antiks. $5-$25.

Two 1.5 inch bull pins, one a longhorn and the other a shorthorn. The third is a bighorn sheep and is a pendant. All three are signed "Razza". These animals and others are also made by Razza in 3-4 inch sizes. These are very nice, quality conversation pieces. Courtesy of Engleberg Antiks. $25-35 each

Gold finish bird pin 2.5" with clear pavé-set rhinestones all over except for the large red open back rhinestone body. Authors' Collection. $35-55

White enamel rooster brooch signed "Pastelli" is example of more expensive choice. Rare. Authors' Collection. c.1950s. $175-225

What The Professionals Kept

The personal collection of professional dealers of costume jewelry, we the authors, reflects the results of our opportunities to find thousands of examples and our personal taste. These are among the jewelry we did not sell but kept to enjoy. They include many fine pieces originally purchased for resale but either we decided not to part with them or we could not sell them for what they were worth. We are still looking, and still buying.

Figural Jewelry

Old fur clip with enamel finish fly sitting on a silver leaf is signed "Monet". c.1940s. $85-95

Small unsigned swan pin with heart dangling from its beak is nicely finished with pave2†set stones in sterling. $75-95

Near 3" lobster pin in sterling with marcasites and very good workmanship. c.1950s. $100-150

Sterling 3.5" moth brooch is signed "Karu". Nice gold wash on metal with large blue rhinestone eyes and clear pavé-set rhinestone body. c.1950s $225-275

Three inch Mazer sterling ballerina with gold wash on body, but silver on dress and head piece. A Quality piece. c.1950s. $225-275

A quality signed Reja sterling lobster brooch nearly 3" long with gold wash front and rhodium back. c.1950s-60s. $275-350

This is the only DeNicola necklace we found in 15 years. It has large purple cabochons, channel set in silver metal. The earrings are Jomaz. The slight color and style difference is not obvious when worn. This is the authors' favorite piece. c.1950s-60s. Earrings $50 Necklace c.$375-425

This picture shows a close up of DeNicola necklace. Note the clear and blue rhinestones are all prong set.

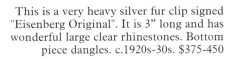

This is a very heavy silver fur clip signed "Eisenberg Original". It is 3" long and has wonderful large clear rhinestones. Bottom piece dangles. c.1920s-30s. $375-450

This is a 3" brooch with double overlaid circles of silver metal covered with clear prong set rhinestones. It is signed "Eisenberg". c.1950s. $250-275

An extra nice 1940s signed Eisenberg set with deep red rhinestones. Look a the perfect match in the design between the necklace and earrings. $450-525

Exquisite is the word for this over 4" Eisenberg Original brooch with large red open back rhinestones. This is one of the pieces that have been the object of counterfeiters. This is the authors' favorite brooch. c.1930s. $600-750

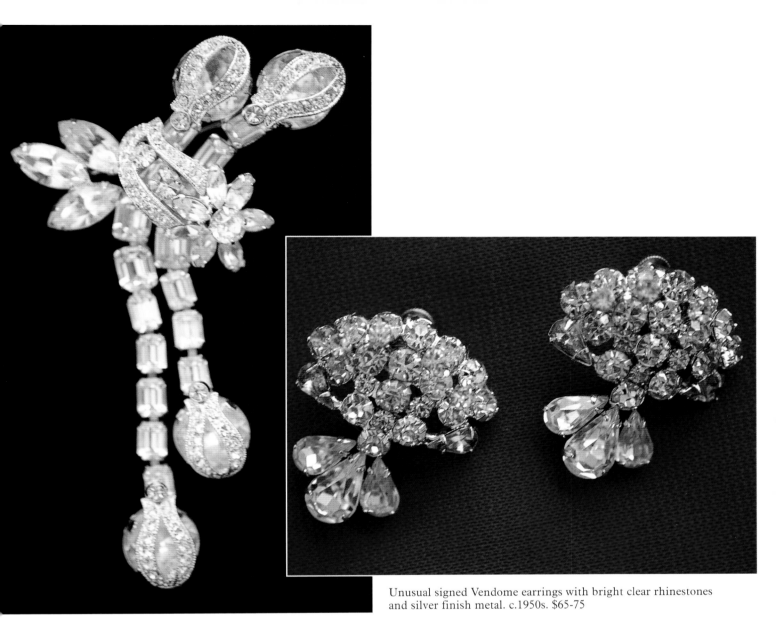

Unusual signed Vendome earrings with bright clear rhinestones and silver finish metal. c.1950s. $65-75

Nearly 5" from top to bottom of this signed Eisenberg brooch with long dangling strands. Large clear rhinestones and quality design make this a fine piece. c.1950s. $225-275

Large green stones surrounded by a row of clear pavé-set stones and finished with a large faux pearl drop form these 2" earrings by Vogue Bijoux. c.1960s-70s $65-75

Very delicate silver metal links lined with tiny prong set clear rhinestones are used to form this elegant, but simple, Kramer necklace with matching earrings. c.1950s. $150-175

Typical fine workmanship is found in this Bogoff necklace with silver metal covered with green and clear rhinestones. c.1950s. $125-150

This 15" necklace is signed "Joseff" in script. It features a gold finish metal with a leaf design and utilizes faux pearls and large channel set rhinestones. c.1950s-60s. $275-325

Signed Craft hinged ram head bracelet is a tasteful combination of black cabochons, clear rhinestones, gold metal and a translucent amber coating. c.1960s. $225-250

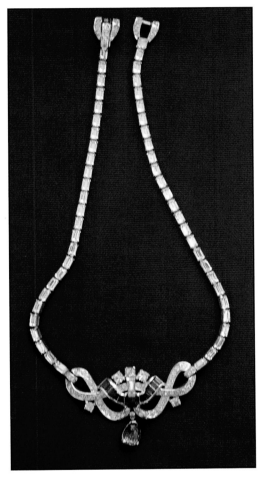

A 15" signed Mazer necklace with very nice clear and blue rhinestones in metal with a heavy rhodium finish. Compare with an unsigned necklace shown at the top of page 79. c.1950s. $225-275

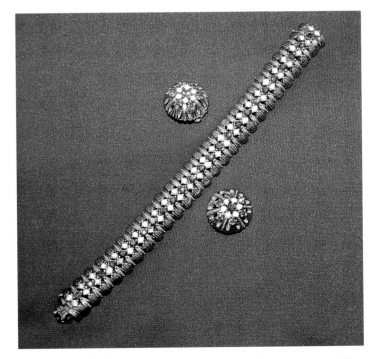

Unsurpassed flexibility is found in this signed Ciner bracelet with matching earrings. Tiny links with green and clear rhinestone in gold finish metal make this a wonderful set. c.1950s-60s. $225-275

This nearly 4" brooch is unsigned but the style and quality might lead one to believe it was a Mazer. It has fine rhodium finish, large green open back stones, and attention to detail. C.1950s-60s. $225-250

Crowns like this 1.75" red rhinestone pin with gold finish metal signed Bauer are popular collector items. c.1990s. $75-95

Typical of Schreiner pieces, this small 1.5" wide brooch is over 1" high in the center. Reverse set light blue rhinestones with larger green cabochons make this an unusual piece. c.1950s-60s. $175-225

A 2.25" Schreiner brooch with clear and champagne colored, reverse set rhinestones, prong set and open back. It is over 1" high in center. Show with matching earrings. c.1950s-60s. $275-350

This matched necklace and earring set has a delicate combination of silver metal design and clear rhinestones. It is a quality unsigned set. c.1940s $95-115

Unsigned bracelet has many unusual shaped silver links with clear rhinestones. c.1950s. $75-125

A 3" unsigned bow pin with clear open back rhinestones in silver finish metal. c.1940s. $75-95

Tiny 1" butterfly is 18K gold with a mix
of different gemstones. $125-150

Basket pin is 18K gold with gemstones. Clear
stones are white sapphires. $150-175

Wonderful lavender colored glass beads with a large
1.5" medallion set in sterling. c.1940s. $125-150

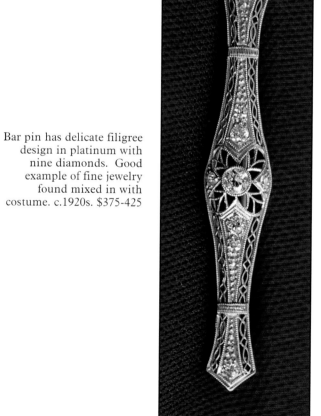

Bar pin has delicate filigree
design in platinum with
nine diamonds. Good
example of fine jewelry
found mixed in with
costume. c.1920s. $375-425

Purple or pink, depending on the light, the glass centerpiece stands out in this slightly japanned filigree Maltese cross pendant. c.1940s. $145-175

This is a 14" sterling link necklace with both square and round crystal stones shown with matching earrings. c.1920s-30s. $145-165

A daintily constructed imported parure with lovely ruby-like rhinestones all prong set in gold finish metal. Origin unknown. $165-185

This unsigned pendant has a nice teardrop shaped cabochon in amber with a reflective a. b. finish. $55-65

A very dainty sterling necklace with a small amethyst cabochon center stone. c.1070s. $75-85

Prong set garnets in sterling, with a 20 inch sterling chain makes this a nice pendant. $95-105

A large 2" carved rose quartz stone with a sterling mount and twisted chain makes up this lovely pendant. $95-125

This is a nice 15" unsigned sterling necklace and 7" matching bracelet. It has a delicate pattern of tiny pavé-set clear rhinestones. c.1930s-40s. Each $85-105

Close-up shows fine workmanship on silver pieces.

An Avid Collector's
Inspiring Choices

Dean Matthews is an avid costume jewelry collector. He began collecting less than fifteen years ago and now has a fabulous collection. He began with the purchase of an unsigned necklace and earrings. He does not restrict his purchases to old costume jewelry or to that of a specific designer, but always buys whatever he finds that he likes. As you will see from the photos in this section, it is usually only the best. At the time the photos were taken, his interests included crown pins, compacts, and newer pieces. A selection of them follows.

As we suggest, Dean wears selected pieces from his collection and displays it all. Chloe, a large stuffed bear, sits on his white sofa wearing ornate pieces.

The rest of his collection is displayed in three large, six-foot, glass-fronted cabinets where pieces are presented on jewelry necks and other display items. It is the best personal display we have seen.

Compacts

Compact is 3.5" navy blue enamel with gold filigree signed "Stratton". $65-95

Compact is 2.75" of silver with hand painted enamel Victorian scene. $250-275

This is Chloe. This bear wears nothing but the best.

Compact is 4", with a geometric design of
enamel over copper. $95-125

Trifari sterling crown pin has gold wash, a row of pearls
across the top and red and green rhinestones across the
base. c.1950s. $225-275

Trifari sterling crown pin with gold wash, large red
and blue cabochons and green baguette shaped
rhinestones across the base. c.1950s. $250-325

Four items: Left is solid perfume, gold with purple enamel sea shell
box, $35-45; right is Estee Lauder 2" purple rhinestone compact,
$125-250; top is solid perfume box with cameo lid. $25-35; bottom
is 2" red enamel compact. $125-175

Trifari crown pin with gold wash metal and two larger red stones inset behind clear pavé-set, and smaller blue diamond shaped and green baguettes across the base. This is a commerative piece celebrating the coronation of queen Elizabeth. c.1960s. $175-200

Small Trifari sterling crown pin has gold wash, two large milky cabochons and smaller red and blue cabochons with green baguettes across the base. 1950s. $175-200

Bellini silver metal crown pin covered with clear pavé-set rhinestones except small green baguettes across the base and a single round rhinestone at the top. $75-125

Weiss crown pin with gold wash metal, two red, and one larger green, cabochons and many pearls, including a row of smaller ones across the base. $125-175

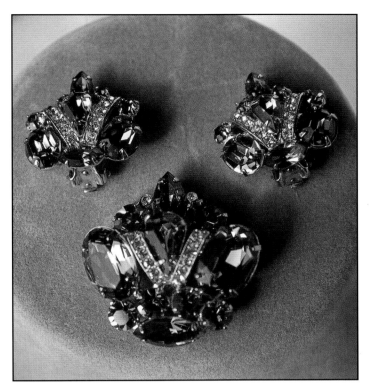

Weiss crown pin and earrings in silver metal with large clear cabochon and various shaped clear and smoky stones. $125-150

Thelma Deutsch over 2" crown pin, with gold finish, has seven smaller size blue cabochons just above a row of purple baguettes across the base. A large lion stands above the crown. It has a small pink rhinestone crown on its head. $125-150

Ora 2" crown pin in silver metal covered with clear pave2†set rhinestones. $75-100

Unsigned crown pin with lovely assortment of multicolor and multi-shaped rhinestones on gold washed metal. $75-100

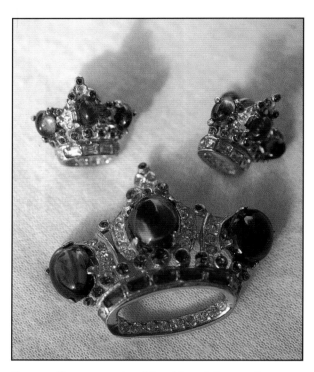

Dorothy Bauer 3.5" wide purple rhinestone crown pin with single strand rhinestone danglers at the bottom, some with stars on the ends. $125-150

Coro sterling crown pin with gold wash has two large green and one large red center cabochon and smaller round red and clear pavé-set rhinestones across the base, comes with matching earrings. $250-275

Three unsigned crown pins: Left pin is open design with red rhinestones around the top edge and a small flower in the center with a row of pink rhinestones across the bottom: right pin has tiny red flowers on gold metal in an open design with seed pearls across the bottom; the bottom pin has and open design with pink, blue, and green rhinestones on japanned metal. $35-85 each

Three newer quality crown pins by Butler and Wilson $150-175

Three unsigned gold crown pins: left has various size cabochons on sides with green center stone surrounded with small pearls; right crown has silver background behind open gold work with small green and topaz rhinestones; lower crown has large purple cabochons on the side and multi color small rhinestones in a delicate pattern. $75-150

Be Patriotic: red, white, and blue crown, pin, and earrings. $75-95

Three Dorothy Bauer crown pins: top is covered with rhinestones in a rainbow of colors; below are small gold pins, one red rhinestones and the other blue. $30-50

Dorothy Bauer green rhinestone
Christmas tree pin with multicolor
decorations. c.2000. $250

Kirks Folly snowman pin.
c.2000. $60

Dorothy Bauer purple rhinestone
Christmas tree pin with multicolor
decorations. c.2000. $250

Kirks Folly red Christmas package with green
ribbon. c.2000. $300

Kirks Folly clear crystal
Christmas tree pin.
c.2000. $250

Patriotic Jewelry

Trifari pin of the American flag waving in the wind. $75

Wonderful Dorothy Bauer 11" bib type American flag necklace red, white, and blue. c.2000 $300-500

Dorothy Bauer 1.75" heart-shaped flag pin. c.2000 $75

Linsa M. enamel finish American flag pin with the flag partially folded is signed "Remember 9-11-01". c.2002. $125

Dorothy Bauer orange and purple butterfly pin $65-75

Dominique multi-color rhinestone butterfly pin with black body. $225-275

Unsigned butterfly pin with very delicate filigree design and various different color rhinestones. $95-125

Unsigned gold metal butterfly pin with many pearls and four pink marques shaped rhinestones. $85-125

Unsigned 4" butterfly pin with silver and clear a.b. rhinestones. $85-125

Unsigned butterfly pin with japanned
metal and red rhinestones. $115-125

Three new unsigned butterfly pins, each a different color $35-55 each

Three new unsigned butterfly pins, each a different color. $35-55 each

Christian Dior set includes a gorgeous 17" necklace with 5.5" long centerpiece and 3.5" matching earrings. It has large round and teardrop emerald color rhinestones surrounded by smaller clear round rhinestones all hand set. c. 1970 $1,500-2,500

Close-up of Dior necklace.

Ballet multi-color art deco parure is striking. It varies in width from 2.75" down to 1" with an invisible clasp and may be worn with the points in various directions. It is shown with long matching earrings. $1200-1600

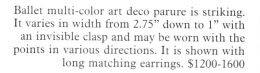

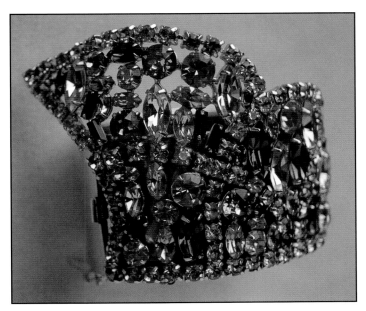

Ballet 2.75" wide multicolor cuff bracelet is part of an absolutely fabulous set!

Korda multi-color rhinestones in brass "Thief of Bagdad" necklace. 1940. $225-275

Hattie Carnegie 2" green enamel panther pin. $125-145

Alice Caviness Swirl design 3" brooch and earrings has all a. b. rhinestones. c.1950s-60s. $175-225

HAR blue sculptured aurora borealis rhinestones, with brown irregular shaped stones used exclusively by this designer, are found in this necklace, bracelet, and earrings (not shown). c.1950s-60s. $475-525

Hattie Carnegie pins: French painter pin with enamel finish; elephant with plastic body, gold metal and pearls; green heart- shaped pin. each $75-100

Florenza gold filigree with three danglers, pearls, and purple and turquoise stones. c.1960s. $65-85

Mazer 2.75" pin is a replica of the golden orb pin from the crown jewels. $225-275

Florenza 7" bracelet with lavender, purple, and green rhinestones. c.1960s. $75-100

The Haskell horseshoe signature on this stick pin, with two shades of purple stones, indicates that it is one of her earliest pieces. $125-155

Dominique necklace set in gold mesh metal with huge centerpiece, 7.5 inches down and across, tastefully decorated with pink, purple, and clear rhinestones. It comes with matching earrings, not shown, over 3" long. This is probably the largest necklace we have seen anywhere. $500-750

Joseff gold finish camel pin with rhinestones in backpack and dangling chains. $325-375

Joseff's gold finish with blue rhinestones decorates this cross pendant. $325-375

Ciner's over 4" long floral brooch with gold leaves is beautiful with red and clear rhinestones on the blossoms. $300-350

Hollycraft's lime green necklace has many rhinestone danglers. 1955. $245-325

Hollycraft 2.25" gold finish pin and earrings with dark and light green rhinestones. c.1950s. $145-165

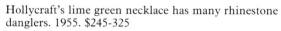

Art Deco 89 necklace and earrings of silver metal squares with ruby red rhinestone centers. $325-400

Hollycraft bracelet has alternating rows of purple, green, and clear rhinestones. 1950s. $95-125

Edlee parure of light and dark blue sculptured rhinestones and some a. b. rhinestones includes a bracelet 1.75 inches wide. $275-325

Sherman, a Canadian designer, clear rhinestone brooch with matching earrings appears to be a grape cluster. $125-145

Florenza purple rhinestone starfish-
shaped pin and earrings. c.1960s. $100-125

Stanley Hagler set has red beaded flowers in a star-
shaped brooch and earrings. $250-300

Stanley Hagler 4.25" brooch has green frosted glass
flowers, tiny seed pearls, and two looped glass
beaded chains. $225-250

St. Johns starburst design set has
japanned metal with pink and clear
aurora borealis rhinestones. $125-175"

Boucher art deco style parure, with extra earrings, has strips of green baguettes separating the clear pavé-set rhinestone balls. $325-400

Stanley Hagler massive red beaded necklace with matching earrings. It speaks for itself. $500-600

Cranberry Hill rhinestone decorated magnifying glass. $50-75

E. Pearl tiger head pin is sterling with extra heavy gold plating. $75-125

Jabot Arabian dagger and scabbard has red enamel, turquoise stones and clear rhinestones. $175-200

A & S triple feather pin from England is made of two tone metal and clear pavé-set rhinestones. $75-100

Bogoff blue rhinestones with overlaid clear pavé-set rhinestone ribbons. $175-200

Bogoff clear rhinestone shield pin. $75-100

KJL pink and red rhinestone slug pin. $75-100

Schiaparelli s-shaped, pink rhinestone, link necklace. $250-300

Kramer bolo style necklace has blue and clear rhinestones. $150-175

Swarovski pear pin has a gold finish with amber and green pavé-set rhinestones. c.1990s. $125-145

"Schiaparelli style" watermelon stones are used in this three piece unsigned set. $300-350

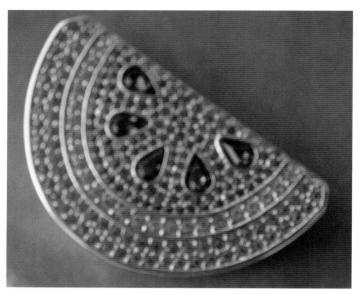

Swarovski gold watermelon pin with pavé-set multi-colored stones. c.1990s. $125-135

ROM gold metal woven basket with delicate amber and green rhinestone flowers. $75-100

Lunch at the Ritz jointed 8" multi-colored enamel and rhinestone dragon pin. Notice the tiny feet under the dragon. c.1990s. $350-400

Lunch at the Ritz 4" jointed multi-colored enamel turkey pin with four rhinestone dangles. c.1990s. $225-275

Sweet Romance rhinestone pins: triangle with tiny rhinestone flowers, flower basket with antique look, and round multi-colored rhinestone pin. $40-50 each

Kirks Folley star fairy wand with moon face pin and two chain danglers. $125-150

Robert 3" brooch has a rhinestone covered bar across the top and from each end hang danglers with balls. The danglers and balls are covered all the way around with rhinestones. $140-180 with earrings (not shown)

Benedict gold pin with four points has a large green rhinestone at the end of each tip and in the center. Nice metal work around the stones. $65-85

105

This large signed Eisenberg Original fur clip is still near perfect with its lovely clear and purple stones. c.1930s. $425-475

Beautiful contrast between green and clear stones was used to make this Eisenberg Ice parure. c.1980s. $375-425

Reverse side of Eisenberg shows fur clips and older pot metal.

Many large rhinestones of different colors with smaller pavé-set clear rhinestones and pearls were used on this gold finish Eisenberg Ice 3" brooch with matching earrings. It was a special Christmas edition in the 1990s. $327-375

Older pink and clear signed Eisenberg parure with 16" necklace (with extender), 2.5" brooch and 1.5" earrings. c.1950s. $400-450

Purple and lavender rhinestones were combined in this signed Eisenberg parure. c.1950s. $400-450

Purple and hot pink prong set rhinestones with small clear paveé-set stones are used on this 7" signed Eisenberg bracelet with matching earrings. c.1950s. $225-275

This Eisenberg Ice 3" brooch is part of the Classic series from the 1990s and has a fine sterling/rhodium finish as setting for floral design. $175-200

Red and hot pink Eisenberg Ice bracelet, 3.5" long brooch and dangle earrings make up this parure. c.1960s. $325-355

Deep purple and lavender rhinestones, with clear rhinestone ribbons, form this 2.75" brooch with matching earrings signed "Eisenberg Ice". c.1960. $250-275

This set consists of a 2" brooch and matching earrings with medium blue and lavender rhinestones signed "Eisenberg". c.1950. $225-275

Eisenberg Ice square brooch has clear prong set rhinestones with very large center stone. c.1960. $150-175

This large signed Eisenberg brooch utilizes two shades of blue rhinestones. c. 1950. $125-175

Older 1960s Eisenberg Ice hot pink necklace is shown with large complimentary 1.75" Ice hoop pierced earrings from 1990s. Set $225-275

This is a clear and ruby red, rhinestone Eisenberg brooch and earrings. c. 1960. $150-200

Quality shows in this large Hobé parure including an 18" necklace, 3.5 inch brooch and matching earrings with large purple rhinestones throughout and small clear pavé-set rhinestones on silver ribbon overlays. $500-600

Lavender and clear prong set rhinestones on silver metal were used in this Hobé 14" necklace and bracelet set. $225-275

This Hobé parure has shiny green enamel on the dainty patterned leaves with gold finish and a large round cabochon center stone. $175-225

Hobé blue frosted glass hinge bracelet has identically matching brooch. $225-275

Trifari pink rhinestone plum pin has leaves of clear pave2†set rhinestones in silver finish metal. $145-175

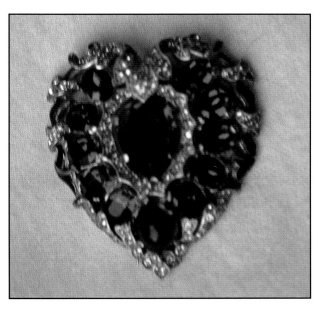

Trifari heart shaped fur clip has silver metal and large green rhinestones. c.1920s. $275-325

Older Trifari 2.5" branch with heavy gold finish has large green rhinestones and tiny clear rhinestone flowers with green centers. $175-225

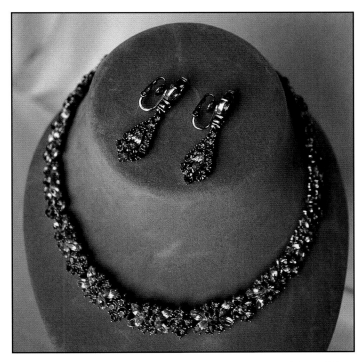

Trifari amber and yellow rhinestone choker length necklace with 1.5" matching earrings. $125-145

Trifari emerald green and navy blue rhinestone choker length necklace with matching bracelet and earrings. $150-200

Quality design was used in this signed Weiss brooch of silver metal and bronze and yellow prong set rhinestones. $145-175

Twisted gold mesh neck chain, lined with a row of aurora borealis stones, has multi-colored rhinestones making up the medallion of the pendant, believed to be an unsigned Weiss. $95-105

Two beautifully designed signed Weiss brooches with many shapes of lovely, blue, prong-set rhinestones. Each $75-95

Rhinestone-lined strand holds this colorful necklace, shown with matching earrings. It is unsigned but believed to be by Weiss. $125-150

This is a wonderful purple, lavender, and hot pink rhinestone brooch signed "Weiss," with matching earrings. $115-145

Very nice design and quality construction were combined in this signed "Weiss," blue rhinestone necklace and earrings. $200-225

This signed Weiss is a high quality set with a 3" purple, lavender, hot pink, and clear rhinestone brooch with matching earrings. $165-185

An older signed Weiss green and clear rhinestone set with necklace and matching earrings. $200-250

Weiss large, square, prong-set, clear rhinestone brooch. $55-75

The bottom pin is an old English style scepter signed Coro Craft. The other is a sterling silver sword pin, unsigned, but believed to be by Coro. Each $125-175

This is a Coro duette consisting of two enamel finish and clear pavé-set rhinestone bird fur clips on a pin-back frame. $275-325

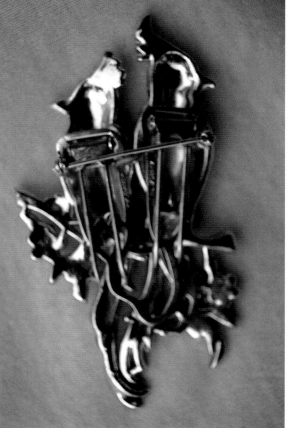

Back of duette shows fur clips and pin back frame.

Quality workmanship went into this heavy gold plated, over 3", Coro brooch with two large flowers. Pink stamens were a tasteful touch used to complete the brooch. $175-225

This Coro Craft bird pin is covered with multiple colors of rhinestones including a wonderful combination of red and clear on the tail feathers. $100-125

This is a wonderful large parure with 26"necklace, bracelet, pin, and 3" long earrings. Large rhinestone frogs are on each link and the full length of each piece. It is signed "Dorothy Bauer," c.1990s. $500-600

Frog shown in close-up of earring.

Large Dorothy Bauer flower basket brooches of multi-color rhinestones have wonderful detail in the flowers and woven basket. c.1990s. $230-250

This Dorothy Bauer pin/pendant cross has an antique silver finish and rhinestones in a lovely flower design. c.1990s. $150-175

Bronze Dorothy Bauer rhinestone owl pin. c.1990s. $45-55

Large rhinestone daisies in multi-colors on a long Dorothy Bauer necklace are spectacular. c.1990s. $225-350

Long 3" Dorothy Bauer brooch with red rhinestone flowers and green rhinestone leaves. c.1990s. $300-350

Whimsical rhinestone pins by Dorothy Bauer: orange hat $40-50, matching sunglasses $25-30, amber purse $65-75, purse pin/ pendant that opens. c.1990s. $95-105

Whimsical rhinestone pins by Dorothy Bauer: red hat $45-55, ruby slippers $40-50, music bar $65-75, red, white, and blue, heart $75-85, and cornucopia. c.1990s. $85-95.

Heavy, full- size, working handcuffs by Dorothy Bauer come with a key and decorated with rhinestones. c.1990s. $375-400

Dorothy Bauer, ice-cream-cone-shaped, jeweled ring box $400; Antique, silver finish, rhinestone, flower basket ring box. c.1990s. $300

Dorothy Bauer picture frame has clear rhinestones around edge and pink and red rhinestone hearts at the corners. c.1990s. $200

Multi-colored rhinestones of many sizes and shapes appear in a 3.5" wide Butler & Wilson crab pin. c.1990s. $225-275

Multi-colored rhinestones are used by Butler & Wilson in this 5.5" peacock pin. c.1990s. $225-250

Large golden rhinestone Butler & Wilson brooch of a parrot sitting in a silver ring has multi-colored rhinestones in the wing and tail feathers, many of which are marquise shape. c.1990s. $225-250

Two blackamoor pins with clear rhinestones and colorful enamel work by Butler & Wilso. c.1990s. Each $150-175

Wonderful gold metal highlights with an array of red, blue, and clear rhinestones make this 5" Butler & Wilson pin an eye catcher. c.1990s. $150-175

Lawrence Vrba magnificent faux pearl finish necklace set with a centerpiece 4" across and 7.5" long, and matching 3" earrings. c.1990s. $500-600

Dominique custom made new parure with large red and clear rhinestone necklace and matching wide bracelet and earrings. $625-750

Unsigned fur clip with blue, orange and yellow flowers on a background of clear rhinestones. c.1930s $65-85

Unsigned, two-dimensional, multi-colored rhinestone, hot air balloon pin. c.1990 $45-75

Heart shaped Austrian brooch with pink, blue, and clear rhinestones, and tiny clear rhinestone flowers around the outer edge. $125-150

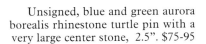

Clever, unsigned, green rhinestone pin with a pearl whiskered cat head pin. $55-75

Unsigned, blue and green aurora borealis rhinestone turtle pin with a very large center stone, 2.5". $75-95

121

Unsigned, gold finish 1.75"
dragonfly trembler pin. $25-35

Lovely unsigned bow is over 3"
long and is completely covered
with pavé-set clear rhinestones
on a silver metal. $100-125

Unsigned, enamel-finish cardinal
and cockatiel bird pins. Each $35

Unsigned, 4" long, dragon pin
with multi-colored rhine-
stones. c.2000. $45-75

Unsigned, unusual overlay construction is utilized in this bright orange parure of necklace, earrings and cuff bracelet. c.1950s. $275-300

Stunning, unsigned, purple and clear rhinestone parure with two-dimensional design. c.1950s. $300-375

Unsigned, pink frosted and aurora borealis clear rhinestone parure, including two-dimensional flower design on the cuff bracelet. $300-375

Unsigned, bib necklace and 2.5" long earrings of clear and ruby red large teardrop overlaid rhinestones are prong set. $250-350

Unsigned brooch, bracelet, and earrings of wonderful blue rhinestones that have other colors inside. $125-150

Unsigned, clear rhinestone necklace with large single tear drop center stone shown with long dangle earrings. $150-175

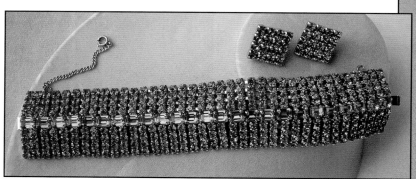

Unsigned, 8" long by 1.5" wide, amber bracelet with matching 1.5" wide square earrings. $125-150

Unsigned and wonderful, this 4.25" long dangle brooch and 2.25"long earrings of clear rhinestones have large, emerald green center stones. $150-200

Unsigned pin and earrings appear to be covered with brass pineapple like pieces with green rhinestone tips. $135-150

Older unsigned pendant with realistic bronzed leaves surrounding a purple rhinestone center and border. $325-375

Unsigned pins: one of clear rhinestones with silver metal finish, and the other of shield shape with clear rhinestones around a pale blue center stone. $50-75 each

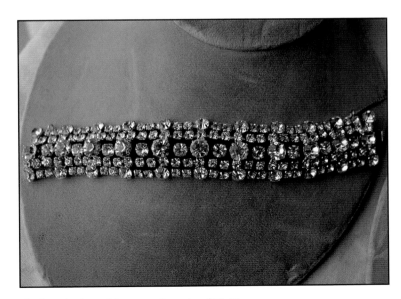

Unsigned, clear rhinestone bracelet. $65-75

Unsigned, Austrian pin is 2.5" long with lovely blue stones and gold dangling chains. $100-125

Unsigned pins: small flag and bird on nest. $45-55. Lion pin signed "Attwood" from England. $125-150

Unsigned, long orange dangle earrings. $45-55

Notice the mask in the centerpiece of this unsigned, red and clear rhinestone necklace shown with complimentary earrings. $100-125

A Passionate
Collector's Broad Interests

Barbara Satalino has been a passionate collector of costume jewelry for over ten years. Her first purchase was the exotic phoenix bird by Marcel Boucher. It is over 4" high with blue and green cabochons and the workmanship and settings make it appear to be fine jewelry. At the time, she had no idea who the designer was, but was intrigued by the piece. She purchased it for $75, which today is approximately one tenth of its value.

Barbara prefers vintage pieces and has collected a large number of Marcel Boucher's designs. Of course, like most collectors, she did not restrict her purchases to one particular designer or category. She broadened her interests to include collecting vintage hats, vintage designer clothing, and accessories. As her interest in collecting these items evolved, she became an active dealer and has done this for several years.

She prefers to display her pieces by wearing them and is usually seen adorned in her favorite pieces. She has, however, shown and displayed her jewelry collection at many venues, including a local historical museum.

Boucher gold carnation pin with a clear rhinestone center. c.1960. $75-125

Marcel Boucher Jewelry

This phoenix bird brooch by Boucher was Barbara's first acquisition. It is over 4" long with blue and green cabochons. The workmanship and settings make it appear to be fine jewelry. $600-800

Boucher sterling cyclamen flower pin has pierced gold and silver finish with clear pavé-set rhinestones. c.1940. $175-225

Boucher flower pin in gold metal, with multiple blue cabochons cascading from one side, and a long funnel shaped rhinestone covered stamen on the other. c.1950s. $255-295

Large Boucher deco brooch with gold finish has red rhinestones across the middle and at the tip of the dangler. c.1950s. $250-300

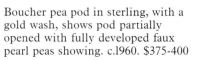

Boucher leaf pin in gold has a lovely center of green and sapphire cabochons. c.1950s. $125-150

Boucher pea pod in sterling, with a gold wash, shows pod partially opened with fully developed faux pearl peas showing. c.l960. $375-400

Boucher sterling vermeil jonquil brooch shows the flower, with clear rhinestones on the tip of each petal, upturned at the end of a turned, gold metal stem. c.1940s. $125-195

Boucher flower has gold petals with turquoise tips and a long pavé-set clear rhinestone stamen. $125-150

Boucher calla lily blossom pin and earrings are finished in both silver and gold. c.1960s. $175-200

Boucher dahlia pin is finished in gold with clear pavé-set rhinestones on the tips of the multi-layered gold petals. c.1950s-1960s. $125-145

Boucher feather pin is finished with silver and gold alternated to show the quills with clear rhinestones at the tip. c.1950s. $95-125

Boucher sterling Deco pin, finished in both gold and silver, has lovely green baguettes. The design reminds one of a sea shell. $175-200

Boucher gold trumpet lily flower pin, with clear pavé-set rhinestones. c.1950s. 125-175

Boucher necklace is lined with gold metal shells with turquoise cabochon centers. c.1960s. 275-325

Boucher brooches: Two are silver covered with pavé-set rhinestones and the appearance of grass waving in the wind. The other is a silver leaf covered with clear rhinestones and ruby red rhinestones at its base. c.1940s. each $150-200

Three Boucher enamel pins: lobster, tropical fish, and fish with pearl on tail. c.1950s. $125-200 each

Boucher designed both the necklace and the earrings shown together, but are not a set. They compliment each-other with clear baguette and pavé-set rhinestones, silver metal, and quality workmanship. c.1950s. $350-450 for both

Boucher graceful bird in flight brooch is finished in gold and silver metal with clear pavé-set rhinestones. c.1960. $95-125

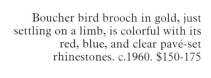

Boucher bird brooch in gold, just settling on a limb, is colorful with its red, blue, and clear pavé-set rhinestones. c.1960. $150-175

Three Boucher pins: gold frog with turquoise plastic body, basset hound, and two giraffes with their necks entwined. c.1950s. $95-175 each

Five Boucher gold pins: Twin swan pins with black enamel on their bodies, three birds with turquoise stones are sitting in a nest, bird on a limb with emerald pavé-set rhinestones body, and a bird in flight in two-tone gold. c.1950s. $95-125 each

Three Boucher gold dog pins: a poodle, a scottie, and a dachshund. c.1950s. $75-125 each

Three Boucher gold animal pins: a Kuala bear climbing a limb, a rabbit, and a squirrel playing with a pearl. c.1950s. $75-150 each

Three Boucher gold pins: a whimsical roadrunner, a grasshopper ready to hop, and bees hovering around a honeycomb. c.1950s. $75-150 each

Three Boucher two-tone gold pins: a bow, a pineapple with pavé rhinestones, and a graceful ballerina. c.1950s. $75-150 each

This Boucher necklace begins with a woven rope of tiny green and amber glass beads supporting a gold and silver feather medallion that supports a large emerald green teardrop. c.1960s. $350-450

A Boucher figural brooch and a choker with alternating turquoise and gold metal beads. c.1960s. $250-350

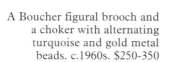

Figural Jewelry

Three butterfly pins: Unsigned with pastel colored rhinestones in open pattern of gold metal; tiny Norway sterling with white opaque enamel; Large blue wedge shaped body and good open work wings. Norway $125-175. Others $50-70

Three unsigned butterfly pins: Green rhinestone with gold edges is from Austria; clear rhinestone pin has round and marquise stone; the bottom pin has pink and red round and marques a.b. stones. Pink and red. $95-125. Others $50-75

Two 2.25" unsigned butterfly pins: one has pink and lilac rhinestones on gold metal; the other has light green and blue on silver metal. c.1960s. $90-150

Three signed butterfly pins: Weiss has amber, topaz, and smoky rhinestones on gold metal; Eddie Green, at top, has slightly raised gold wings with various colored rhinestones around the tips; Kramer has clear marquise and round stones. Eddie Green $30-50. Others $95-125

Unsigned 2.25" long butterfly pin has a wonderful assortment of green and citrine and opalized cabochons in a delicate pattern. c.1950s $125-150

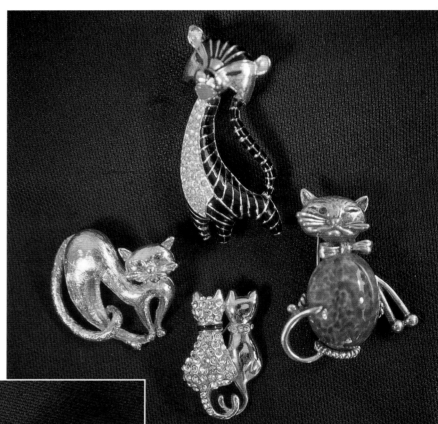

Four unsigned cat pins, all with gold metal: the left has arched back. $25-40; the large cat at top has clear pavé-set stones and black enamel. $30-50; the bottom has two cats, one clear pavé rhinestones and the other gold metal. $30-50; the right is gold metal with a large green stone body. All c.1950-1960s. $25-40

Four beetle pins: large beetle at top left has faux pearl body on gold metal. $50-75; the darker beetle on the right has a tortoise-shell body. $50-75; the lower left is sterling with gold wash and illegible signature. $75-125; the lower right has faux pearl body and turquoise stones in wings. $30-40

Three feline pins: the gold metal cat on the left is sitting up holding a bone. $50-75; the pin at the top is a lion. $75-95 ; the tiger with a clear pavé rhinestone face, on the right, is a signed "Jomaz". $95-125

A fox and two cat pins: fox is sitting up, holding a faux pearl, c. 1960s; cat on right has a mother of pearl body and is signed "Coro," c.1940s; cat at bottom signed J.J. has goggle eyes and a fur body., c.1960s. $50-125 each

Two gold metal pins: top beetle is covered with faux pearls. $30-50; the bottom grasshopper is by Kenneth Lane from the 1970s. $75-95

Two bugs and a spider pins: unsigned large red body. $30-50;
Czechoslovakia spider is all red with wire legs. $30-50; bottom bug is
by Hollycraft from the 1950s. $50-75

Large unsigned squirrel pin of gold metal with a
large green cabochon body and pavé-set green
rhinestone tail. c.1960s. $75-95

Three gold metal bird pins: Orange enamel bird on limb by nest
is signed "J.J."; penguin is all gold metal; bird holding a dangling
metal heart. $25-40 each

Three owl pins with gold finish: top wearing glasses is signed "J.J."; green-eyed owl, bottom left, is a signed Jomaz; owl at right is an older K.J.L. $60-80 each

Two Rooster pins: small gold metal with many pearls is signed Hobé. $125-175; the larger rooster has an enameled finish with open foil-back citrine and amber rhinestones. $90-125

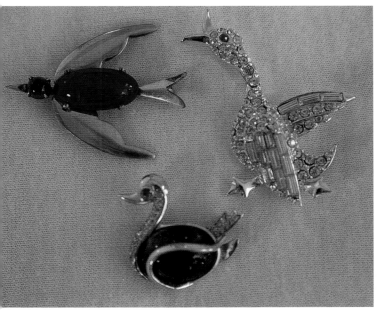

Three bird pins: Top left by Trifari is a bird in flight, gold metal and a brown scarob body; right is unsigned clear rhinestone duck; bottom is a duck with gold-filled metal and a green stone body. $40-75 each

Four turtle pins: large white enamel pin, on the left, with clear rhinestones is by Marvella. $95-125; gold turtle, at top center, with green and clear rhinestones is sterling by Trifari, pat. pend., c.1940s. $125-175; turtle, on the right, with the enamel design on the is by DeNicola from the 1960s. $125-150; gold turtle, lower center, is unsigned. $50-75

139

Unsigned 3" turtle pin with watermelon pink rhinestone body is covered with rhinestones. c.1950s-60s. $95-125

Two fish pins: the upper unsigned pin is gold metal with black and white enamel. $50-90; the lower signed K.J.L. has antique gold finish and clear pavé-set rhinestones on the face. $75-125

Two unsigned turtle pins both in gold metal: One on the left has a topaz rhinestone shell and the other has a tortoise-shell cabochon body. $50-95

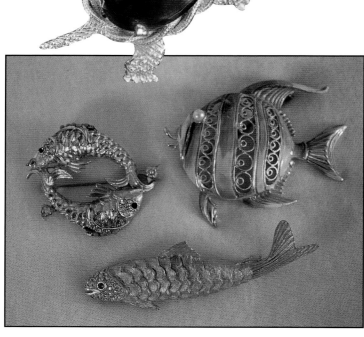

Two unsigned turtle pins one covered with peridot rhinestones and the other a moonstone with clear rhinestones surrounding it. c.1960s. $90-125 each

Three unsigned fish pins with gold finish: the two fish swimming in a circle chasing a pearl; the large fish has enamel work and a pearl eye; the long fish has clear rhinestones on the face and detailed scales in the metal. c.1950s-60s. $40-70

Large unsigned mechanical clown pin has a faux pearl head and body with black rhinestones in legs and arms. $125-150

Two enamel pins: The orange enamel mushroom is unsigned; the purple plum is signed "Kramer." $75-115 each

Two scarecrow pins in gold metal: the unsigned pin on the left has multi-colored rhinestone shirt and green cabochon face with chain dangles; the other is signed "J.J." and has a faux pearl face with detailed straw work in the gold metal. c.1950s-60s. $90-130 each

This is an unsigned red bakelite pear with a large heavily gold plated leaf. c.1930s. $300-400

Unsigned gold finish pin has two turtle doves
sitting on the branch of a tree. $75-125

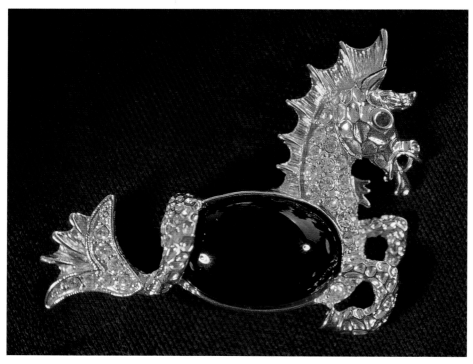

K.J.L. seahorse pin has detail in the gold metal and a large emerald
green, cabochon body. c.1980s. $95-125

Signed Jewelry

Miriam Haskell poured glass purple beads
surround the neck and a lovely medallion
of tiny beads and gold metal creates a
beautiful delicate design. c.1940s-50s.
$400-600

Miriam Haskell bells, bells, and more bells completely line the necklace and
cascade down from the clip earrings. c.1950s. $400-600

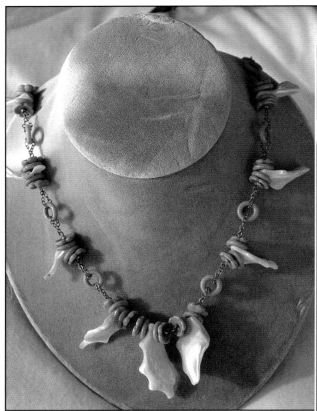

Miriam Haskell necklace is lined with irregular shaped pieces of mother of pearl, turquoise and coral that increase in size with the largest at the front. c.1950s. $250-350

Miriam Haskell pendant has attractive gold neck chain and medallion with large red glass cabochon set in gold metal, makes it a stunning piece. c. 1950s. $300-400

Miriam Haskell designed this gorgeous 4" long tortoise-shell flower-shaped brooch that has three dimensional construction. c.1940s. $300-400

Miriam Haskell, two strands of faux baroque pearls hold a lovely floral medallion made mostly with tiny seed pearls. c.1940s. $600-800

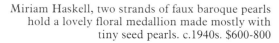

144

Vogue put heavy gold petals behind dainty wires tipped with multi-colored rhinestones and finished this brooch with several large rhinestones in the center. c.1940s. $150-200

Miriam Haskell out-did herself when she designed this lovely necklace with two strands of faux baroque pearls and a 3" by 6" gold leaf, seed pearls, and large pearl medallion with five drops of faux pearl dangles. c.1940s. $600-800

J. Feinberg butterfly pin has a delicate design of multi-colored rhinestones. $175-250

Vogue moth pin has gold wings and green rhinestones with a large European cut faux amethyst body. $175-250

Pauline Rader lion pin with gold finish and large blue cabochon mouth is completed by a mane of several woven chain dangles with gold tips. c.50s-60s. $95-125

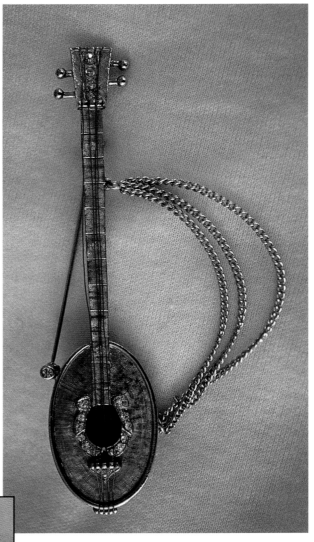

Mandel
l sterling mandolin pin is 4" long and has dual gold and silver finish with three draped gold chains. $150-195

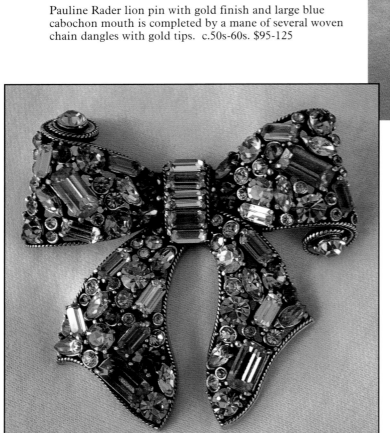

Hollycraft 3.5" by 3.5" bow brooch in multicolor rhinestones of many shapes is a wonderful example of the designer's workmanship. This color combination of rhinestones was used almost exclusively by Hollycraft. Dated 1957. $375-400

Hollycraft octagonal brooch, dated 1951, has citrine round and oval rhinestones set in gold metal. $95-150

Hollycraft twin flower pin, with pastel aurora borealis glass petals and four bead danglers, is an unusual piece for this designer. c.1950s. $95-125

Schiaparelli designed this long gold leaf pin with a cute red frog, with kite shaped blue rhinestone legs and pearl eyes, sitting on it. c.1960s. $95-125

Vendome brooch has very unusual color and shape rhinestones completed with three faux pearl danglers. c.1960s. $95-125

Schiaparelli 7" bracelet with alternating gold and white marbled cabochon stone links is complete with safety chain. c.1960s $150-175

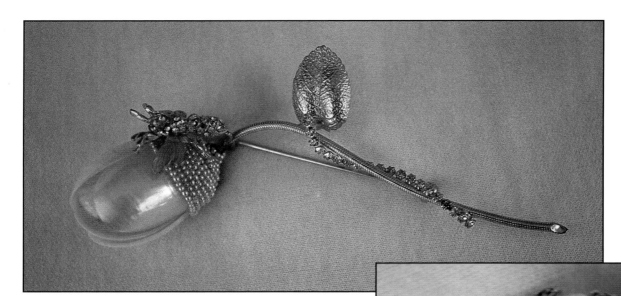

Rosenstein 6" pin has a very nice rose finished in mother-of-pearl with tiny faux seed pearls around its base and a tiny bee. c.1940s-50s. $300-400

Ciner flower brooch, from the 1950s, has perfectly formed flowers and leaves in antique gold with turquoise cabochon centers. $175-250

Hattie Carnegie pin looks like an island native with its turquoise and blue plastic body and gold metal skirt, is complete with a clear pavé-set rhinestone headband.

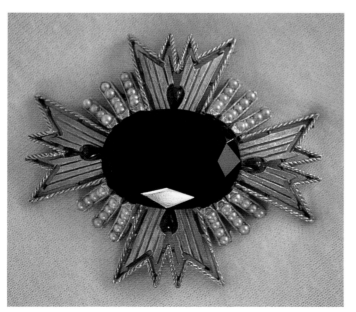

Art designed Maltese cross pin with gold finish has a wonderful 1.25" dark green rhinestone center, small pearl and green stone accents. c.1950s. $75-125

Art pear shaped pin with matching earrings in gold metal is covered with various size peridot aurora borealis rhinestones. c.1940s 150-175

Art flower blossom pin with earrings has gold and silver filigree metal petals with japanned center. c.1950s. $125-175

Coro multiple layer gold finish insignia brooch has unusual design with an opened winged eagle and tiny crown in the center. c.1950s. $90-125

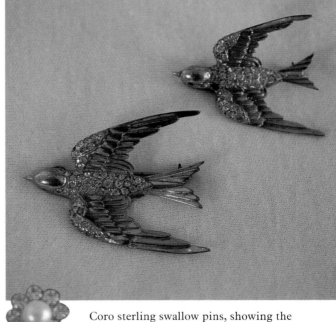

Coro sterling swallow pins, showing the birds in flight, have a light gold wash with some pavé-set clear rhinestone highlights. c.1930s. $75-125 each

Coro sterling rose gold wash flower basket pin is one of the designer's finer pieces. The basket is full of dainty flowers with a mixture of faux pearl, turquoise, and green rhinestone centers. c.1940s. $125-175

Napier set with shaped leaves of various shades of silver filigree metal and small metal balls to break up the design. c.1950s. $200-275

Reinad 4" lily brooch, in sterling, has light gold wash except on parts of the flower petals where clear pavé-set rhinestones are found. c.1940s. $300-400

Yves St. Laurent parure is large with clear Lucite links separating round gold links with smoky cabochon centers. c.1970s. $400-500

Trifari is known for its "jelly belly" pins made in the 1930s, named from the clear Lucite bodies. This pin is an excellent example, still in mint condition, depicting a Pekingese dog. Note the enamel work and clear pavé-set rhinestones. c.1930s. $1500-1800

Trifari "jelly belly" penguin with gold metal and rhinestone accents. c.1930s. $1200-1500

Trifari piece designed by Diane Love. It is a bronze metal mask replica of the Okame goddess of mirth. $300-500

Crown Trifari flower fur clip has three tones of gold metal and a clear rhinestone stamen. c.1920s. $200-300

Trifari pat. pending lily brooch has three lilies with green rhinestone centers, clear pavé-set rhinestones, and green enamel stems. c.1940s. $150-200

Napier seahorse brooch in gold metal is covered with amber and champagne rhinestones. $65-75

Janney 3.25" long Maltese cross pendant has a dark blue confetti aurora borealis cabochon center. c.1950s. $125-150

Small, Mandell lamb pin is composed of small gold circles and completed with blue eyes. c.1950s. $50-75

Kramer 2.25" long clip dangle earrings in silver metal are shown with an unsigned clear rhinestone necklace with similar design and stones. c.1950s. earrings $75-125. necklace $100-125

Trifari "jelly belly" pins are signed and dated in the 1990s. $90-170

The Show Must Go On, by David Mandell, 6" long, cat pin is a theatrical piece, custom made, using clear rhinestones set in silver metal with green rhinestone eyes and pink rhinestone ears and mouth. c.1990s. $300-400

Hobé Oriental water carrier pin is completely covered with peridot- and topaz-colored rhinestones. c.1950s-60s. $125-175

Miriam Haskell pendant with gold chain of heavy strands and long over 6" medallion in matching gold design with clear rhinestones and large faux pearl drop. c.1940s. $250-350

Miriam Haskell choker of gold speckled black faceted and yellow trumpet glass beads. c.1950s $400-500

158

Unsigned Jewelry

Unsigned set has lovely floral design. Each daisy-like flower is made of five glass petals with amethyst centers and amethyst colored leaves in the background. c.1960s. $300-500

Unsigned necklace with red glass and pearl beads supporting a fringe of clear and red rhinestone crystal dangles. c.1960s. $400-500

Unsigned 5" by 3.5" butterfly is wonderful with its fragile filigree design in silver, with a multitude of different shapes and colors of rhinestones. c.1940s-1950s. $350-395

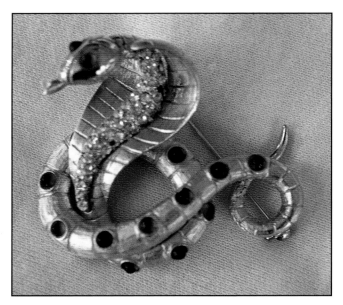

Unsigned coiled cobra pin in gold, with multi-colored rhinestone spots. It appears ready to strike. $95-125

Unsigned lion pin has black face and red eyes, with some detailed enamel work. $125-175

Unsigned elephant head pin looks ready for the circus parade. Made of gold metal, the ears are finished in black enamel and a large red rhinestone decorates its forehead and headpiece. $125-175

Unsigned brooch with two branches. It is striking with one branch covered with clear rhinestone buds and the other in full bloom with cranberry red stones. $275-325

This is an original headpiece from England. It consists of a gold metal framework with clear, prong-set rhinestones. c.1920s. $500-600

Unsigned and beautiful is the only way to describe this layered amethyst rhinestone brooch with large amethyst center stone. $95-125

Unsigned Oriental water carrier pins look well worn separately or together. Finished in gold with blue enamel vests, they carry bead water containers. $125-175

Unsigned, two-dimensional faux pearl pear pin is completed with tiny carved glass leaves set in gold metal frames. $250-275.

Unsigned Austrian brooch is 3" wide by 6" long. The top bow bends with the weight of the woven gold chain and four dangling gilded filigree balls decorated with multi-colored enamel. c.1950s. $200-300

Unsigned pins all finished in enamel: a butterfly, a pelican, and an orchid.

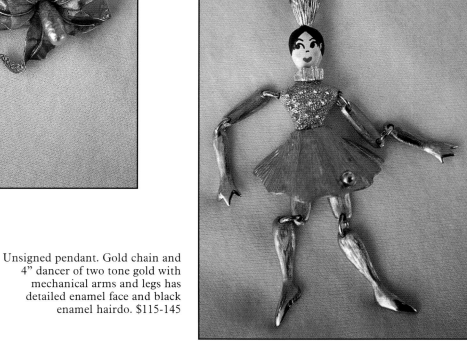

Unsigned pendant. Gold chain and 4" dancer of two tone gold with mechanical arms and legs has detailed enamel face and black enamel hairdo. $115-145

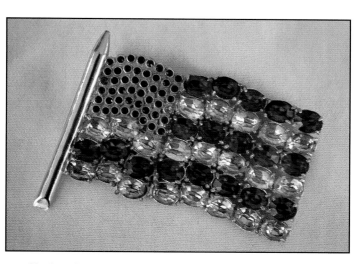

Unsigned American flag brooch in gold metal shows its age with only 48 stars. $125-175

Unsigned, expensive looking, flamingo brooch has rose gold metal and a large amber rhinestone body. c.1940s. 175-250

Unsigned sterling chatelaine-type sweater brooch in gold consists of two separate pins connected by two gold chains. On one pin, a single bird is flying; on the other, two birds sit on a tree limb. $150-195

Unsigned large, pink, tropical bird brooch shows wonderful design and destail using an enamel finish. $75-125

Czech flower brooch has many layers of gold filigree metal with a variety of large, different colored rhinestones. c.1920s. $75-125

Unsigned designer necklace has a thick twisted neckband of multiple strands of tiny faux pearls and a medallion consisting of various size large pearls, crystal beads, and rhinestone-covered balls. c.1960s. $500-600

Unsigned, beautiful, 4" long, three-toned rose gold spray brooch tied with a bow. Flowers are large, multi-colored rhinestones. c.1940s. $150-200

Unsigned rose pin and earrings set has petals of gold metal with turquoise bead centers. c.1970s. $45-95

164

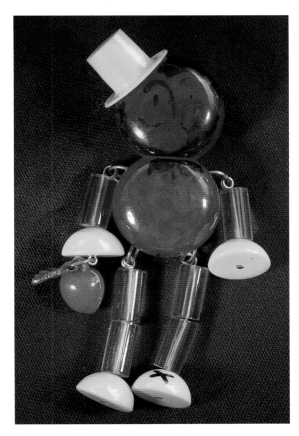

Large, unsigned, crib toy made of multi-colored Bakelite. c.1930s. $100-200

Unsigned small bib necklace is made of silver metal and large round clear rhinestones. c.1950s. $150-200

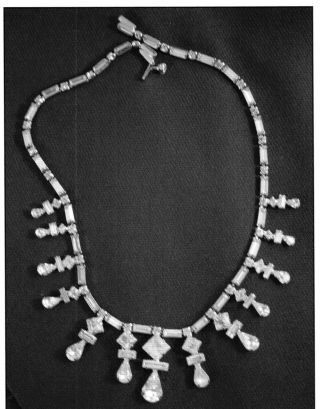

The danglers on this unsigned necklace are made of clear tear-drop and baguette rhinestones, while the unusual chain is clear baguettes. c.1950s. $75-125

This long, clear rhinestone necklace, with a fish design, is very unusual. c.1950s. 125-175

Unsigned 3.5" long bow is elegant, with silver and heavy gold wash metal and ruby red and clear rhinestones. c.1940. $150-190

Unsigned clear rhinestone pins: one is a pinwheel design made of clear round prong set rhinestones. c.1950s. $90-125. The other, a dangler, is 4.25" long, made from clear, marquise, prong-set rhinestones. c.1950s $90-125.

Unsigned half-moon shape brooch has marquise-shaped clear rhinestones in silver metal. c.1950s. $50-75

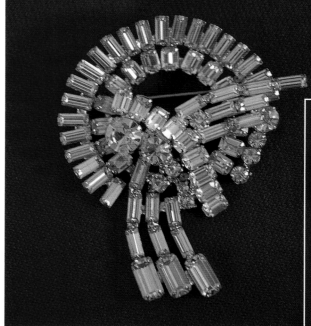

Unsigned round brooch of clear baguette rhinestones has a cascading spray across and below. c.1950s. $95-125

Three unsigned, clear rhinestone brooches: Left, a round, dome-shape with sunflower design. c.1930s. $125-150. Right, an oval-shaped rhinestone pin. c.1950s. $125-150. Bottom, a wreath-shaped pin. c.1950s. $75-90

166

Unsigned, 3.25"long, cross pendant in finely decorated gold metal with large citrine and topaz prong-set stones. c.1960s. $125-150

Unsigned, 4" long, cross pendant in gold metal with green rhinestones and a large green cabochon center stone. c.1950s. $125-150

Unsigned, 4" long, cross pendant in antique gold finish with multi-color round, oval, marquise, and baguette aurora borealis rhinestones. c.1950. $125-150

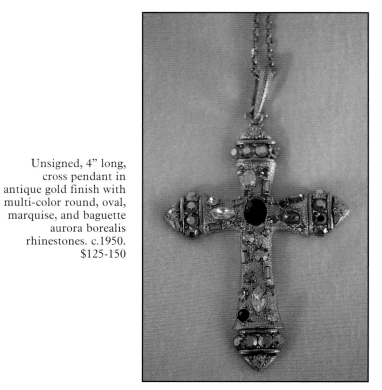

Unsigned, clear rhinestone pins: Left: square design with a floral center of rhinestones in wonderful, assorted cuts. c.1940s. $125-150. Right, a leaf design with clear prong-set rhinestones. c.1950s. $75-125

This unsigned tiara has a high front of clear, prong-set rhinestones. c.1950s. $125-200

Three pairs of unsigned clip earrings: one is round with a large clear rhinestone center stone. A second square and a third triangle- shaped pairs both have clear and black rhinestones. c.1940s-'50s. $95-150

Two pairs of unsigned clear rhinestone dangle earrings 3.25" long. c.1940s-50s. $150-200 each

This unsigned brooch is sterling silver with a variety of different sized round, diamond- cut, clear rhinestones. c.1950s. $75-95

This unsigned, 1.5" wide bracelet in silver metal has round and baguette clear, prong-set rhinestones arranged in square patterns. c.1950s. $150-200

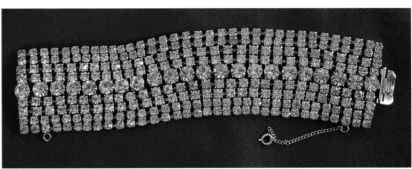

This unsigned, 1.75" wide bracelet in silver metal has round, prong-set rhinestones. c.1950s. $250-275

Unsigned, 4" long, butterfly brooch with brushed gold wings and blue rhinestone body sitting on a large floral branch consisting of one leaf and three flowers with brushed silver petals. c.1950s. $125-150

The signature is illegible on this bib-style necklace with multi-colored, prong-set rhinestones and aurora borealis border. c.1950s. $400-500

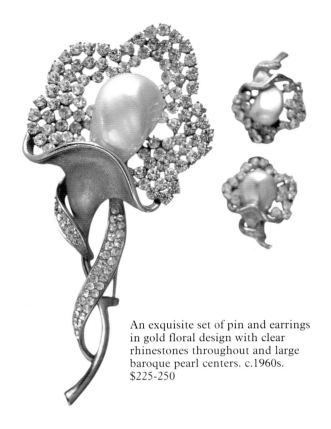

An exquisite set of pin and earrings in gold floral design with clear rhinestones throughout and large baroque pearl centers. c.1960s. $225-250

Unsigned, rigid necklace has five large gold nuggets, each with an oval, pale pink, center stone. c.1960s. $300-400

Unsigned pendant necklace of glass beads with a marching drop medallion. c.1960s. $125-175

Unsigned choker has large tear drop faux pearl dangles and identical pieces combined with smaller round pearls to complete the medallion and neckband. c.1970s. $250-350

Wide, unsigned, fringe choker has large, round, flat, blue, aurora borealis beads alternating with round, silver metal beads. All the metal is slightly japanned. c.1960s. $200-300

Three strands of large baroque pearls hold an over 6" long medallion of three pierced gold pieces with fringes of the same large pearls and a small barbell-shaped decoration made of tiny pearls. c.1960s. $350-400

This lovely, expensive-looking necklace is formed with gold, leaf-shaped, metal pieces covered with clear, pavé-set rhinestones. c.1960s. $250-325

Unsigned, bow choker with flexible gold metal neckband and large gold bow with black, emerald-cut stone in the center. A lovely wide, purple rhinestone, and gold metal bracelet. c.1940s-1950s. Choker $300-400. Bracelet $175-250

Clean
Display, and Protect

Keep It Clean

Cleaning costume jewelry is essential whether for a collection or for resale. Some of the best buys we ever made were when we bought costume jewelry that was filthy. These pieces must be examined carefully and are always a gamble but are often worth it.

If you have a piece of jewelry that is reasonably clean but the stones are a little dull and it needs to be refreshed, try something simple. Often at shows we would purchase a piece in this condition from a private party and wanted to display it immediately. We would simply hold the piece near our mouth and gently blow our breath on it. The slight bit of moisture did not damage anything. We would then wipe the surface with a jewelers' cloth, or a piece of flannel material, and bring it back to life.

Cleaning jewelry with closed-back stones

Remember, when cleaning costume jewelry with rhinestones that are closed back, the worst enemy is getting them wet and having moisture get behind the stones. It will cause the foil back on the rhinestone to deteriorate and the stones will turn black. Avoid dipping these pieces. If they are really dirty and need it, use a soft toothbrush that has been slightly moistened with a window cleaner. This will usually do the trick. Hold the piece so that no liquid runs behind the stones. Immediately lay it, face down, on a towel and use a hair dryer, on a low heat, to remove any moisture.

When cleaning jewelry with closed back stones, we suggest you avoid the small machines made for cleaning jewelry. Our experience with these was that the cleaning was excellent but within a few days the stones would begin to darken.

Cleaning jewelry with open-back stones

Most of the costume jewelry, that does not have closed back stones, is not as likely to be damaged by moisture. You can again use the soft toothbrush and window cleaner or even warm soapy water to clean these and can rinse them in warm water. It is best to gently shake them and dry them with a soft cloth and the hair dryer right after the cleaning. If the open back stone has a foil back, be extremely careful not to damage the foil.

Cleaning jewelry without stones

Silver and copper metals are usually best cleaned with a jewelers cloth and, if necessary, a tiny amount of a cleaner specifically designed to clean these surfaces. Faux pearls and beads can normally be cleaned with a little soap and water but you want to be gentle and avoid soaking them as the string may be old and could break and you will have to repair them. A tiny bit of Tarnex® cleaner on a soft toothbrush will remove the green mold often found on the findings between the pearls.

Keep It Handy
Storing a collection or inventory

After your jewelry is clean and you want to put it away for safekeeping, remember, to avoid the moisture. Rhinestone pieces should not be stored for long periods in plastic bags unless the tops are left open. Place your excess jewelry that you don't wish to display, in jewelry boxes or perhaps between material layers in a larger box or dresser drawer. Since we were once dealers, we store ours in one of the cases that hold multiple trays made for jewelry display. If you are a dealer and will be moving the jewelry frequently we recommend the jewelry trays. They allow for quick set up at shows. If you remove the jewelry from the trays, glance to be sure stones are not missing. If stones are missing you may find them in the tray. If practical, it may be best for either collections or merchandise, to store the rhinestone pieces in individual boxes as any stones that become loose and fall out can be easily retrieved and replaced.

Jewelry tray makes ideal storage as all items can be easily seen.

Wearing and displaying a collection

Wear the pieces in your collection as often as possible and you will get a great deal of satisfaction from the compliments you receive. Your cosmetics are your jewelry's worst enemy. Always remember, when you dress to go out, your jewelry goes on last. When you get home, your jewelry comes off first. If it has been raining out, lay the rhinestone pieces on a towel, face down, and dry with a hair dryer on low heat. Some of our customers have displays of parts of their collections in glass top tables, hanging in wall cases and even have individual pieces on display on teddy bears or dolls. Don't stick all of your collection in a box in the closet or you will lose interest and won't enjoy it.

Jewelry trays are ideally stored in jewelry cases which may be made of soft materials or hard as shown. They store compactly and hold hundreds of pieces. About $40

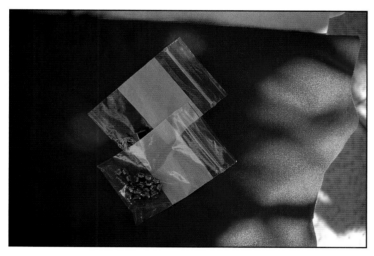

Plastic bags hold individual pieces or sets and they can be seen without opening the bag. Stones that fall out till remain in bag. These create a moisture problem for rhinestone jewelry if top is not left open.

Keep It Safe
Insuring your jewelry

You must give at least some thought to protecting your investment. The first protection is to store it where it will not get damaged. The second is to be certain it is insured. Review your homeowners' insurance policy and see what the limits are on jewelry. After you do this, you should determine about what your collection is worth. Your insurance will usually group this with the gemstone jewelry and even fur coats when figuring your loss. If you want to be covered, you can usually purchase additional insurance at a reasonable rate. To do this, you will need to list the jewelry and may be required to take photos. If you have a scanner attached to your computer, consider laying the pieces face down on it to get the photos. It is low-cost and can produce very good results.

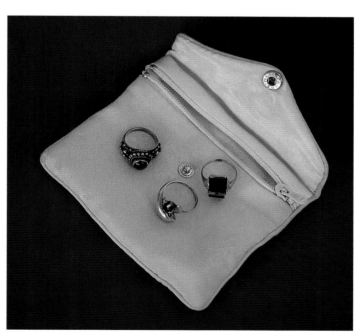

Soft bags provide great protection but must be opened to see what is inside. Might use for special pieces

To emphasize the value of properly insuring your collection, we will end this section with another personal experience. We had a large collection of a wide variety of jewelry and over the years we collected butterfly pins. At one time the collection was over four-hundred pieces. We sold the less expensive ones and kept about three hundred. No two were alike and they were all in perfect condition. Among them were two-hundred signed pins, many were sterling, some of which we paid as much as $300 each. Figuring our pins averaged $75 each in value, our collection was worth about $22,500.

While in the process of moving, we left these in one of our homes. That home was broken into by burglers and all the butterflies were stolen. None were ever recovered. Between our two homeowner policies, we collected $6,000. This recovery included the loss of two mink coats. You should consider insuring your collection. You must decide for yourself.

Our last word is to dealers. Beware, because thieves may follow you when you leave an antique show. They will have seen your merchandise and know what you have. Don't be too tired to be alert, and notice if anyone is following you.

Boxes with cotton provide excellent storage and will sit in jewelry trays. Always use boxes if they are ones that originally came with the jewelry.

Jewelry cases also make good protective storage. They will sit in jewelry trays, but are often too tall.

Recommended Reading

Baker, Lillian. *Fifty Years of Collecting Fashion Jewelry 1925-1975* Paducah, Kentucky: Collector Books, 1986/1989.

Ball, Joanne Dubbs. *Costume Jewelers The Golden Age of Design*. West Chester, Pennsylvania: Schiffer, 1990.

Bell, C. Jeanenne, G.G. *How to be a Jewelry Detective*. Shawnee, Kansas: A.D. Publishing, 2000.

Dolan, Maryanne. *Collecting Rhinestone and Colored Jewelry*. Iola, Wisconsin: Krause Publications, 1998.

Ettinger, Roseann. *Forties & Fifties Popular Jewelry*. Atglen, Pennsylvania: Schiffer, 1994.

_____. *Popular Jewelry 1840-1940*. West Chester Pennsylvania: Schiffer, 1990.

Kelley, Lyngerda and Nancy Schiffer. *Costume Jewelry The Great Pretenders*, West Chester, Pennsylvania: Schiffer 1987.

Miller, Harrice Simons. *Official Identification and Price Guide to Costume Jewelry*. New York: Avon Books, 1994.

Schiffer, Nancy. *The Best of Costume Jewelry*. West Chester, Pennsylvania: Schiffer, 1992.

_____. *Rhinestones! A Collector's Handbook & Price Guide*. Atglen, Pennsylvania: Schiffer, 1993.

_____. *Costume Jewelry: The Fun of Collecting*. West Chester, Pennsylvania: Schiffer 1992.

_____. *Fun Jewelry*. West Chester, Pennsylvania: Schiffer, 1991.

Index of Designers

A

Andersen, David, 14, 16, 17
Art, 56, 68, 70, 150, 151
Art Deco, 89, 99
Attwood, 126
A & S, 102
Avon, 149

B

Ballet , 94, 95
Bauer, Dorothy, 78, 88-92, 115-118
Bellini, 86
Benedict, 105
Bogoff, 76, 102
Boucher, 28, 66, 101, 127-134
Butler & Wilson, 88, 118, 119

C

Carnegie, Hattie, 59, 95, 96, 150
Castlecliff, 152
Caviness, Alice, 95
Ciner, 24, 77, 98, 150
Copper Bell, 17
Coro, 52, 88, 114, 137, 151
Coventry, Sarah, 60
Craft, 77
Cranberry Hill, 101

D

deLillo, 148
DeNicola, 49, 53, 73, 139
Deutsch, Thelma, 87
Dior, Christian, 94
Dominique, 92, 97, 120

E

Edlee, 99
Eisenberg, 7, 12, 25-28, 45-50, 67, 68, 73-75, 106-109, 152
Eugene, 19, 59

F

Florenza, 96, 100
Francios, 152

G

Giovenchy, 58

Gell, Wendy, 60
Green, Eddie, 135
Grosse, 153

H

Hagler, Stanley, 21, 100, 101
HAR, 96
Haskell, Miriam, 19, 21, 55, 97, 143, 144, 158
Hobé, 11, 15, 20, 59, 60, 110, 139, 152, 158
Hollycraft, 48, 54, 98, 138, 146, 147

J

Jabot, 102
Janney, 156
J.J., 137, 139, 141
Jomaz, 7, 25, 136, 139
Joseff, 12, 24, 76, 47, 98

K

Karu, 72
Kirks Folley, 90, 105
Korda, 95
Kramer, 76, 103, 135, 141, 157

L

Laguna, 22
Lane, Kenneth, 102, 137, 139, 140, 142, 153
Lauder, Estee, 85
Linsa, M., 91
Lisner, 153
Lunch at the Ritz, 104

M

Mandell, 146, 156, 157
Marboux, 153
Marvella, 139
Matisse, 18
Mazer, 44, 45, 72, 77, 78, 96, 149
Monet, 71

N

Napier, 60, 154, 155

O

Ora, 87

P

Pastelli, 70
Pearl, E., 101

R

Rader, Pauline, 146
Razza, 70
Reinad, 43, 154
Reja, 72
Renoir, 18
Robert, 2, 19, 105
ROM, 104
Rosenstein, 25, 59, 65, 150

S

Schiaparelli, 103, 147
Schreiner, 65, 66, 78, 148
Sherman, 99
Staret, 67
Stratton, 84
St. John, 100
St. Laurent, Yve, 8, 154
Swarovski, 103, 104
Sweet Romance, 105

T

The Show Must Go On, 157
Tortoloni, 66
Trifari, 8, 85, 86, 110, 111, 139, 154, 155, 157

V

Velstria, Perlana, 14
Vendome, 75, 147, 148
Vrba, Lawrence, 120
Vogue, 145
Vogue Bijoux, 75

W

Weiss, 9, 24, 54, 64, 67, 86, 87, 112-114, 148, 149